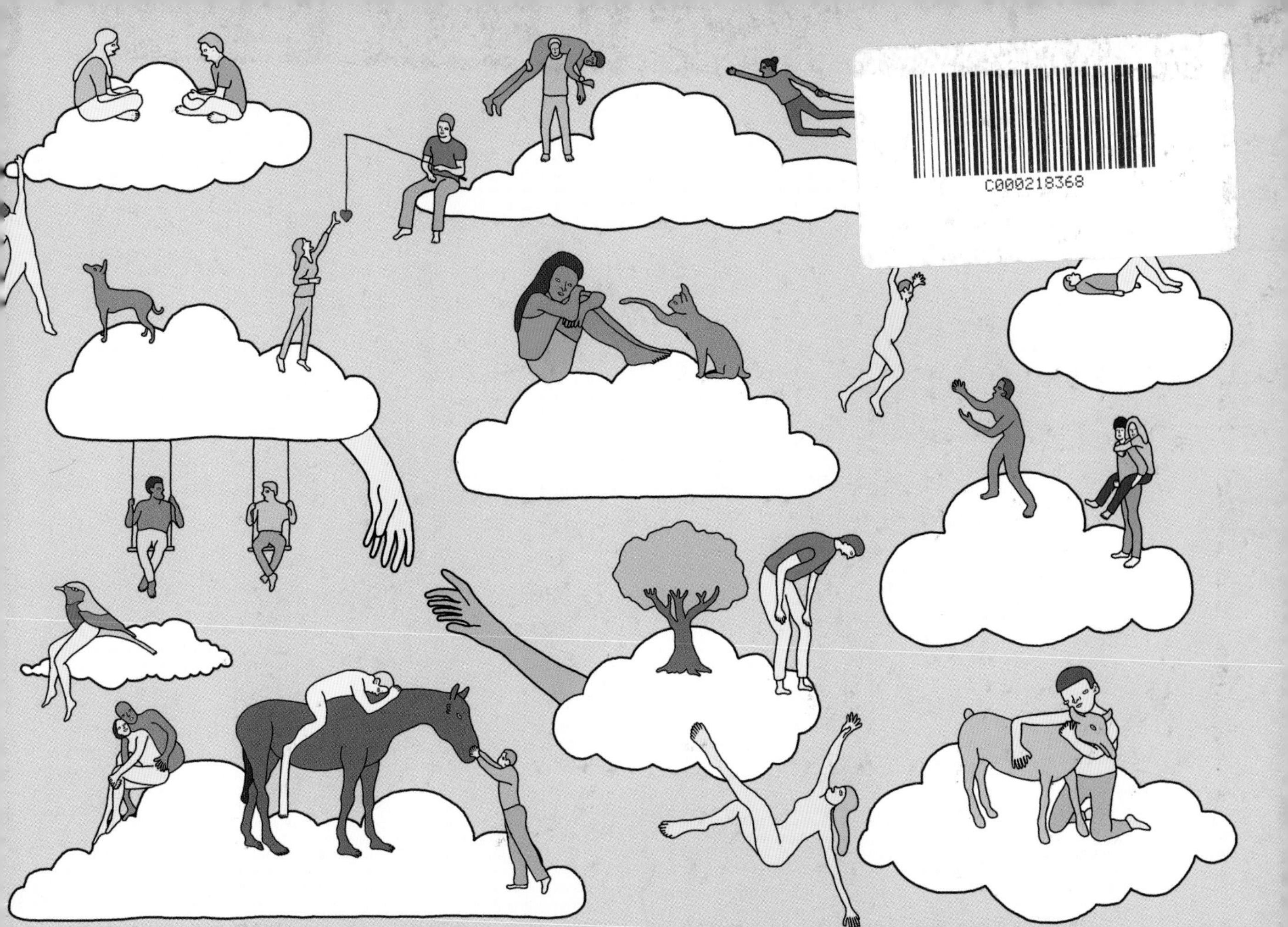

First published in Great Britain in 2020 by Trapeze
an imprint of The Orion Publishing Group Ltd
Carmelite House, 50 Victoria Embankment, London EC4Y 0DZ

An Hachette UK Company

1 3 5 7 9 10 8 6 4 2

A CIP catalogue record for this book is available from the British Library.

ISBN (Hardback) 978 1 409 19711 9
ISBN (eBook) 978 1 409 19742 3

Printed in Italy

www.orionbooks.co.uk

MIX
Paper from
responsible sources
FSC
www.fsc.org
FSC® C023419

how to make friends with strangers and stay friends until you die

a really inspirational guide to friendship

by chris (simpsons artist)

question:
what is friendship

is it this

is it this

is it him

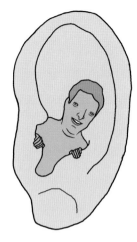

is it this

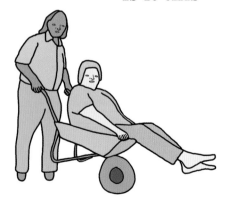

is it them

answer:
friendship is all of these things
it is their presence on a lonely day
a hand when you cant find the way
your laughter when they are sad
their smile when you are mad
their ear when you need to talk
and your wheelbarrow when they cant walk

it is loving someone with every single ounce of your being
and bathing in their love for as long as it shines
upon your heart

why is friendship important

have you ever been lonely and wished there was someone you could talk to or have you ever been stuck inside a wall when you was trying to see if you could fit in between the soft bit of the wall and the bricks only to get your arm and most of your neck trapped and you had to drink your own spit for 9 days so you didnt die well if your answer to this is probably then you have just answered the question of why friendship is important because if we didnt have a friend in our life who we could talk to when we was lonely or rescue us from inside of a wall then we would probably be dead and that would be really sad so having a friend in your life is a important thing for all of us and i hope that by having a read of this book you will learn how to be the number 1 friend that the world has ever known. love from your friend Chris (Simpsons artist) xox

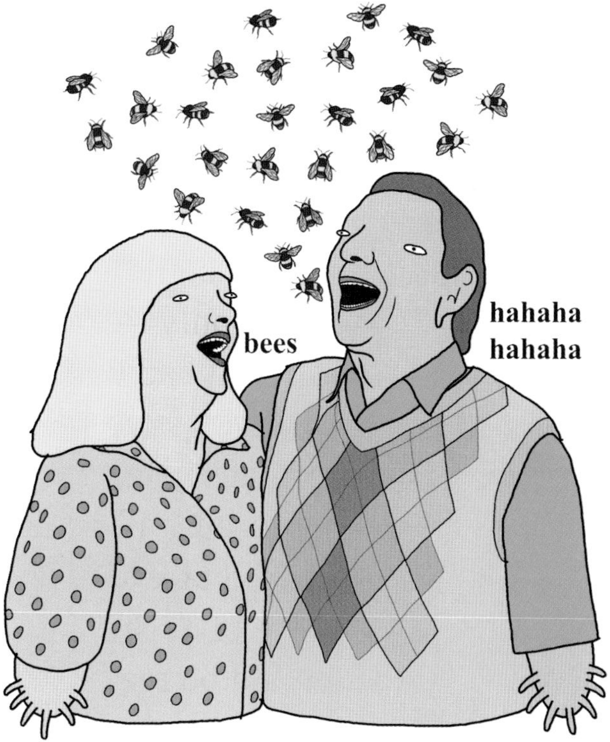
bees
hahaha
hahaha

a true friend is someone
who can make you laugh until
thousands of bees fly out of your mouth

the first founding fore fathers of friendship

wrap your
eyeball
around this

nice

edward friend

pauline ship

the origin of friendship

the earliest known recorded sighting of friendship was on june 23nd 1956
in london england when edward friend met pauline ship in the street
and edward showed pauline a photograph of a wet cloth that had dried
into the shape of a little boy patting a dogs head with a leaf
from this moment on these two men became very close
and would end up sharing their love of cloths dogs boys and leafs
for the rest of their days and friendship was officially invented
and to this very day this is the reason that the 1950s is now
known throughout the world as the golden age of friendship

being alone

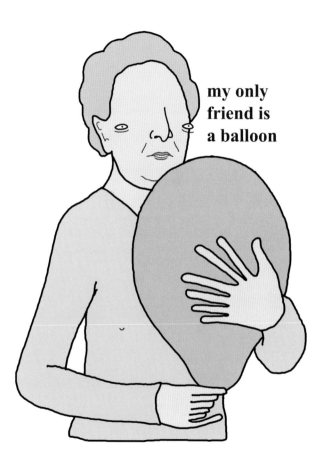

my only
friend is
a balloon

why do you have no friends

there is lots of reasons why you might
not have any friends but the main reasons
are that you are a annoying person or a
show off or a diabetic mess but the most
main reason of them all is not being a
confident person because no one wants
to be friends with a shy guy because that
is like being friends with a balloon and
being friends with a balloon is like
being friends with air and who wants
to be friends with air because air is
completely pointless but once you know
why people dont like you then it is more
easy for you to change the way that
you are so you can have more friends
for yourself

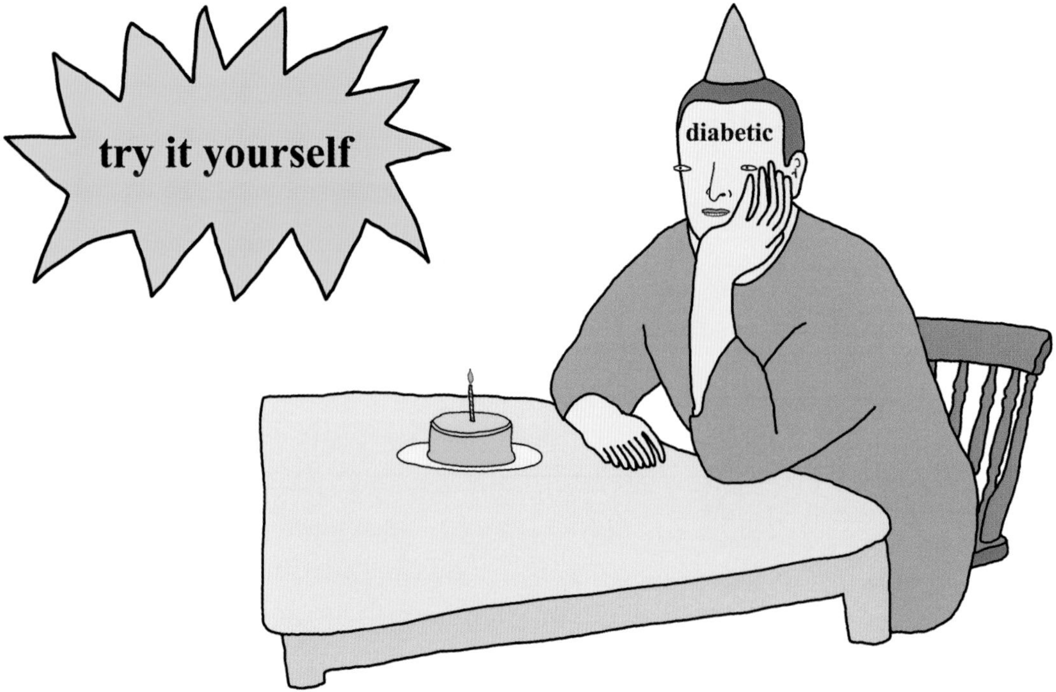
try it yourself
diabetic

a quick 5 minute task for you to do is to think of all of the reasons why people dont like you and then write the most important one on your forehead so you can be reminded of it everyime you look at yourself in the mirror or in the reflection of a puddle

how to make people like you more:
turn yourself into a dog

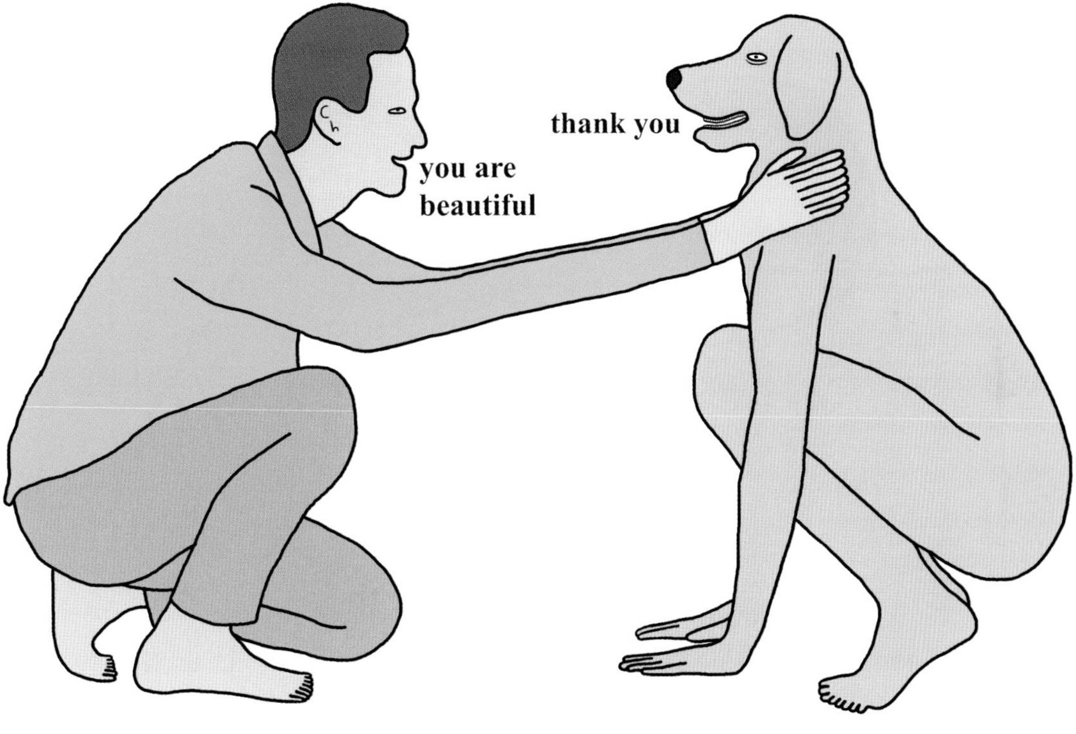
you are beautiful
thank you

how to feel less alone:

fill a glove up with sand and put it on your arm
so it feels like someone likes you
and you are not a pathetic mess

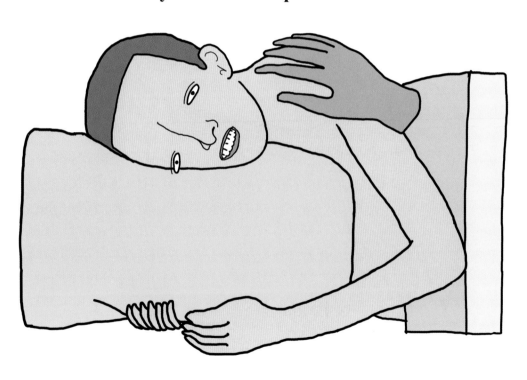

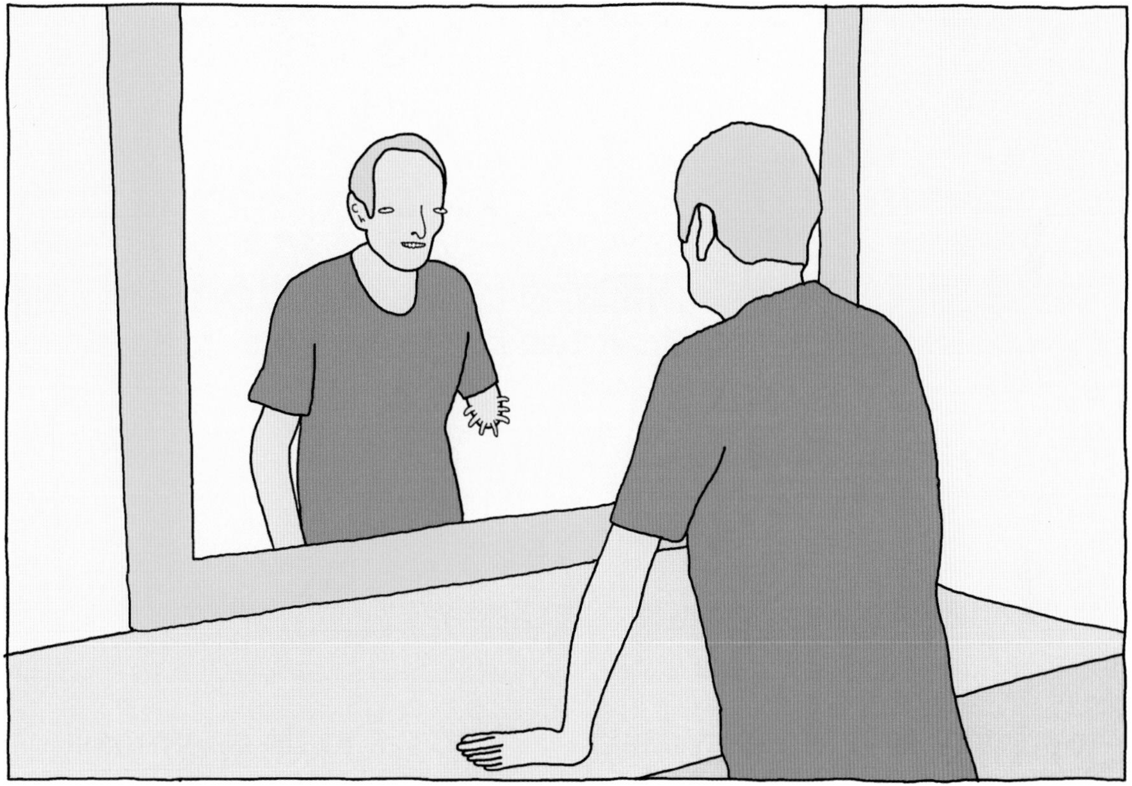

fun things to do when you are alone:
look at yourself in the mirror for 1 hour

building up confidence

a good way to build up your confidence is to do a gymnastics
performance in front of a crowd of people
this will help you to feel comfortable in your own body
and give you the courage to make a friend

smile more

did you know that smiling is a simple way
to make yourself feel more confident

not confident

the most confident

why dont you try out a smile for yourself just now

making friends
with strangers

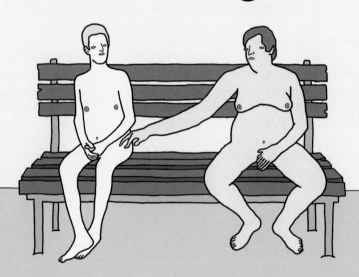

strangers can be found in every part of the world
they are on the bus and in the shop they are in schools
and in offices and near lamposts and even in the woods
no matter where you look you will find a stranger
so that means no matter where you look you will
find a friend who is waiting to be born
and that is a beautiful thing to remember

making friends with strangers might seem like a scary
thing to do but i hope that in this part of my book i will
help you to have a learn all about making friends with
strangers and by the time that you are finished having
a read of it you will feel confident about making
friends with strangers anywhere that you find them

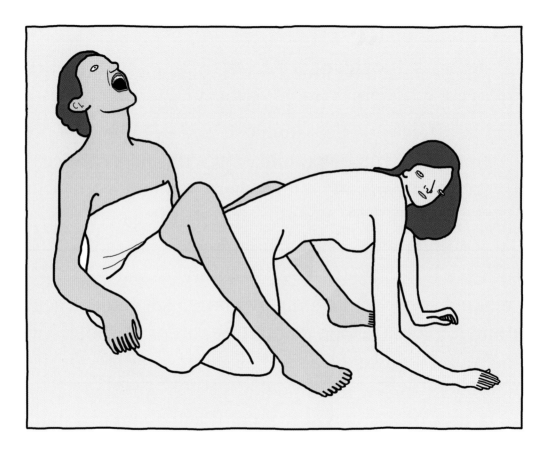

inside every stranger is a friend waiting to be born

how to make friends with strangers:

link toes with a stranger of your choice to show them you are a caring person and you mean them no harm

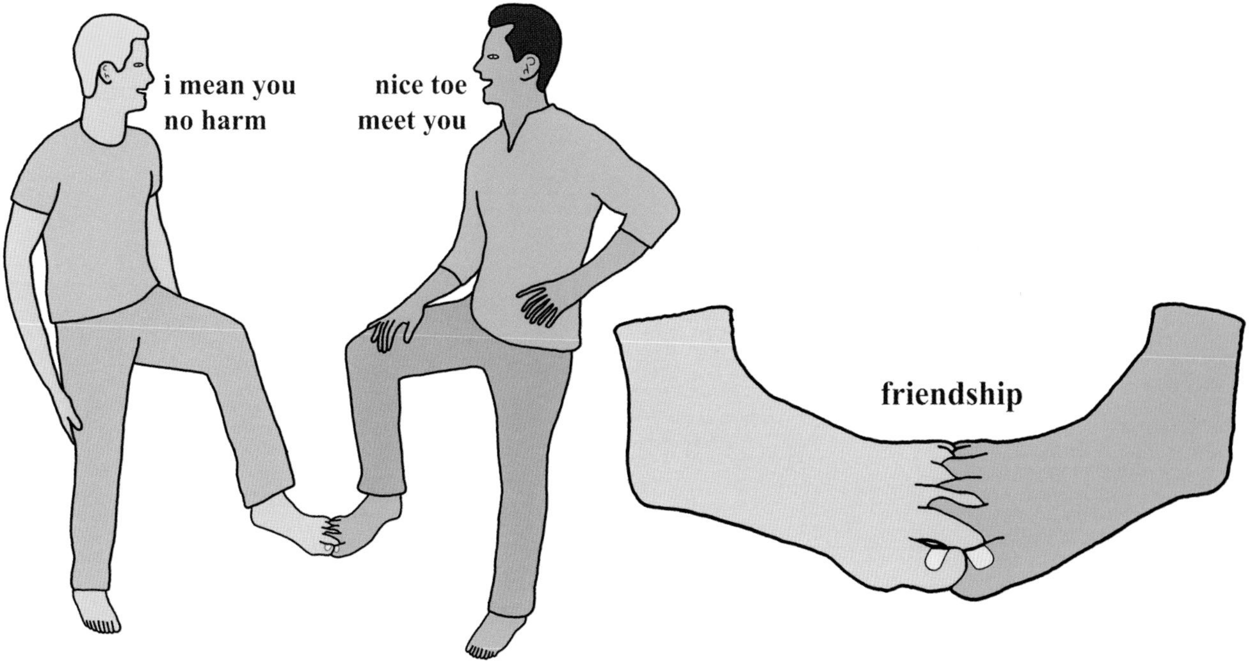
i mean you no harm
nice toe meet you
friendship

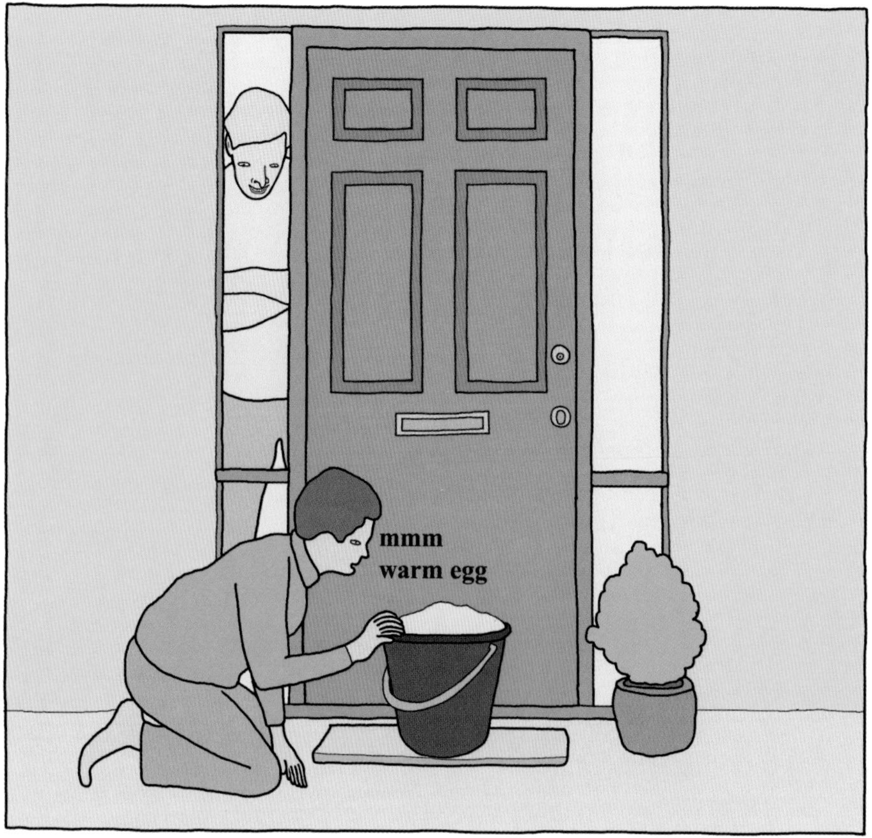
mmm
warm egg

leave a bucket of warm scrambled egg on your doorstep
to lure hungry strangers to your house

if you see someone who is eating lunch on their own at school why dont you sit next to them to make them feel less lonely and then you can become their friend

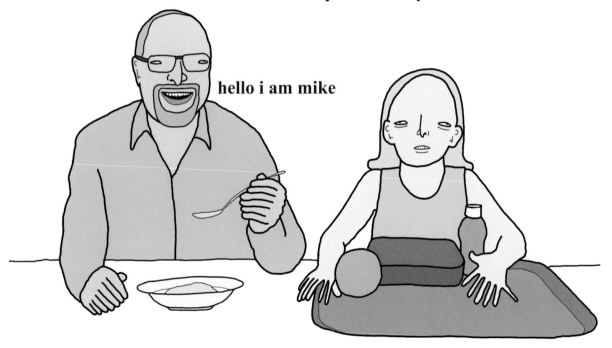

hello i am mike

escalator

gently touching a persons hand on
a escalator is a tender way
to start a friendship with
a stranger

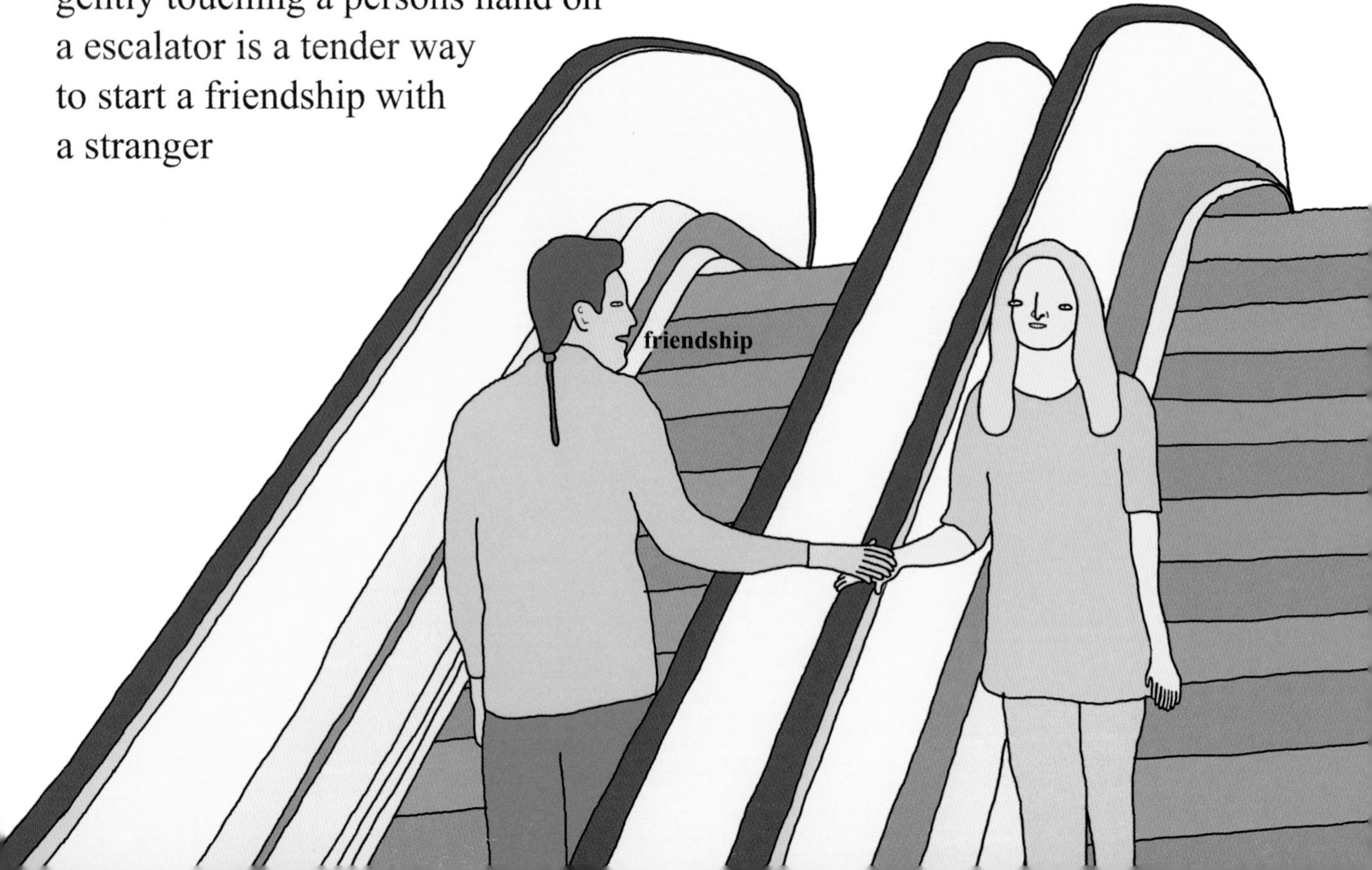
friendship

the tender touch of a stranger

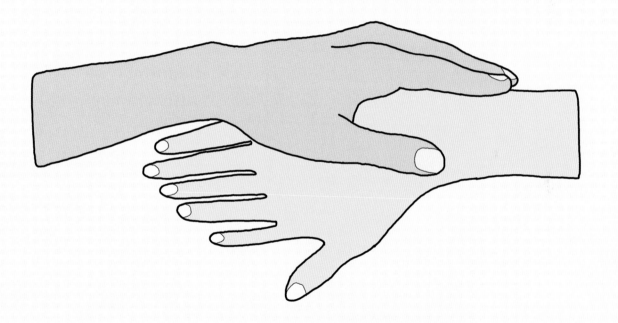

i cried when i was having a draw of this

neighbours

your neighbours are
strangers that you
see every day

become close friends
with your neighbours
by letting them feed
you over your
garden fence

first impressions

it is important to make a good first impression
when you first meet a stranger so make sure
you do something that they will
cherish inside of their thoughts
until the day that they die

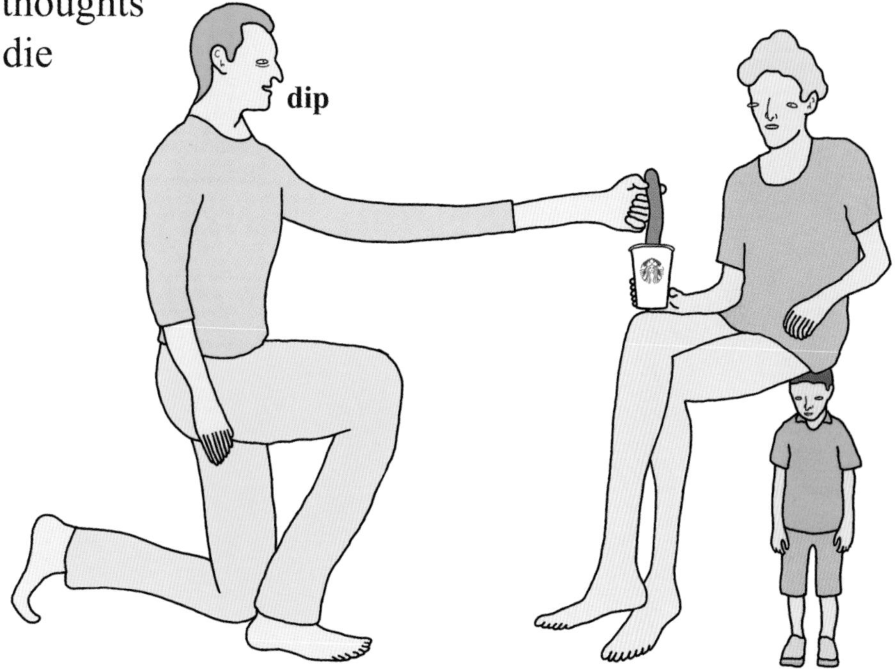
dip

how to make friends with strangers at the gym:
softly kiss a stranger at the gym while they work out
to show them that you like them and you want to be their friend

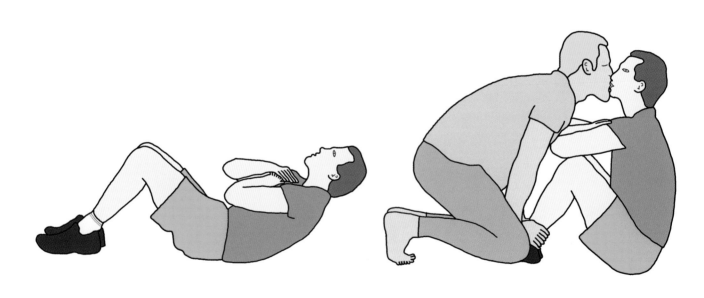

looking for friendship
are you looking to start a
beautiful friendship with a stranger
if your answer is yes
then meet me at this lampost
at midnight when the
bell chimes noon
bring a feather
yes yes yes yes yes yes yes yes yes yes yes yes yes

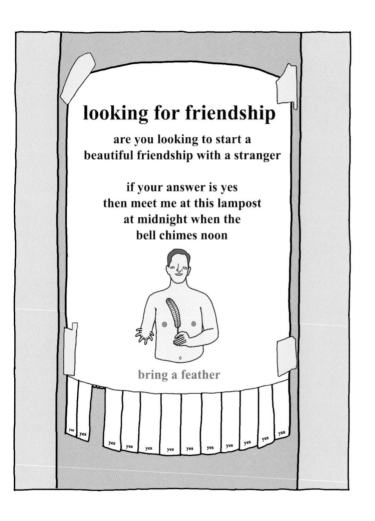

a sign

a great way to meet strangers
is to put a sign on a lampost
offering your friendship
to anyone who sees it

friendship clubs

if trying to make a friend out in the world is a bit too frightening for you then you will be pleased to know that there is places that you can go to make friends with people who have got similar interests as you these places are called friendship clubs

in this chapter you will learn about the main types of friendship clubs that you can go to
so if you dont see a club here that you like then maybe it is time for you to get a new interest
or prepare to die alone

dolphin club

welcome to dolphin club this is a place where you can meet new friends while you show off your dolphin to other men and children dont worry if you dont have a dolphin of your own because you can hire one for £4 a hour at the reception area next to the bins

god he is lovely

thanks so is yours

skateboard helmet club

**now that
is a nice
skateboard
helmet**

people always say to me chris what is the best club
to meet people who have got a interest in
skateboard helmets and without even
thinking i always say skateboard helmet
club because it really is the best club
to meet like minded people who
have got a interest in
skateboard helmets

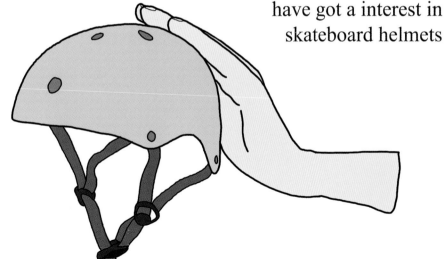

dads romantic film club

everyone loves romantic films even dads so that is why dads romantic film clubs are a good place to meet dads who have got a passion for passion so why not find your nearest dads romantic film club so you can have a watch of a romantic film and chat about it with passion papas who are just like you and who knows you might even meet a romantic dad who wants to have more than friendship he may even want to have a kiss of your hair if you are lucky as well

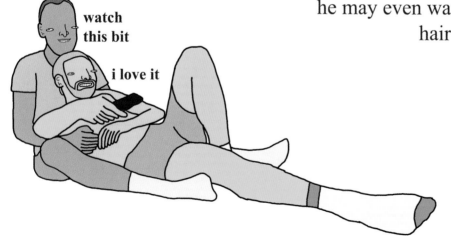

massage club

before technology was invented in the 1980s people would join massage clubs to meet new people and to this very day neck massages are just as popular as text messages as a great way of making new friends and because there is over 900 million massage clubs for you to join in the world you are only ever 4 steps away from a massage club so it is the perfect place for you to make meet and keep new friends

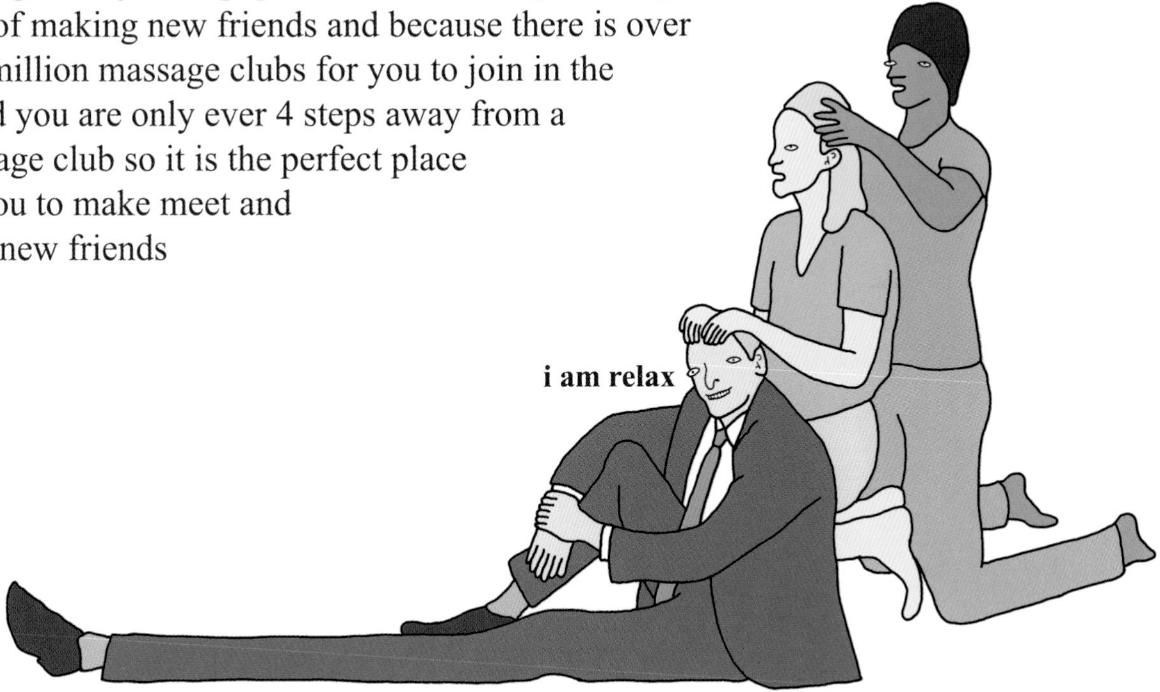
i am relax

horse whispering club

god i love horses dont you they are like massive brown dogs
if horses didnt exist i think i would just kill myself they are so
good i love their hair and their legs and their long ones so that
is why i like to go to the local horse whispering club so i can
whisper my secrets to a horse of my choice for up to 1 hour
and if the horse decides he would like to become friends with
me then i can go and visit him every tuesday or every second
sunday to continue our friendship until the horse dies

**tell me your
secrets my child**

**i cant
read**

egg club

this is my best club that i like to go to when i want to
meet a new friend because there is nothing as
relaxing and laid back as sitting in a room
with strangers and breathing in the smell
of warm wet egg so if you love the
smell and the taste and the feel
of pure egg then this is
definitely the club for
you to meet a
new friend

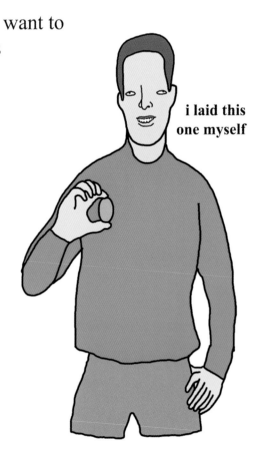

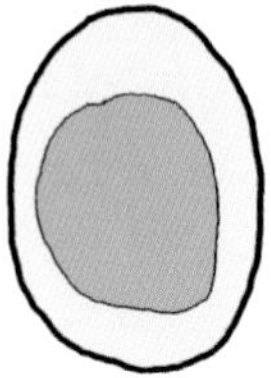

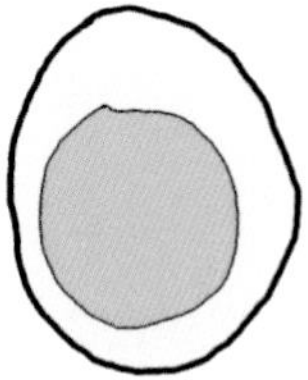

i laid this
one myself

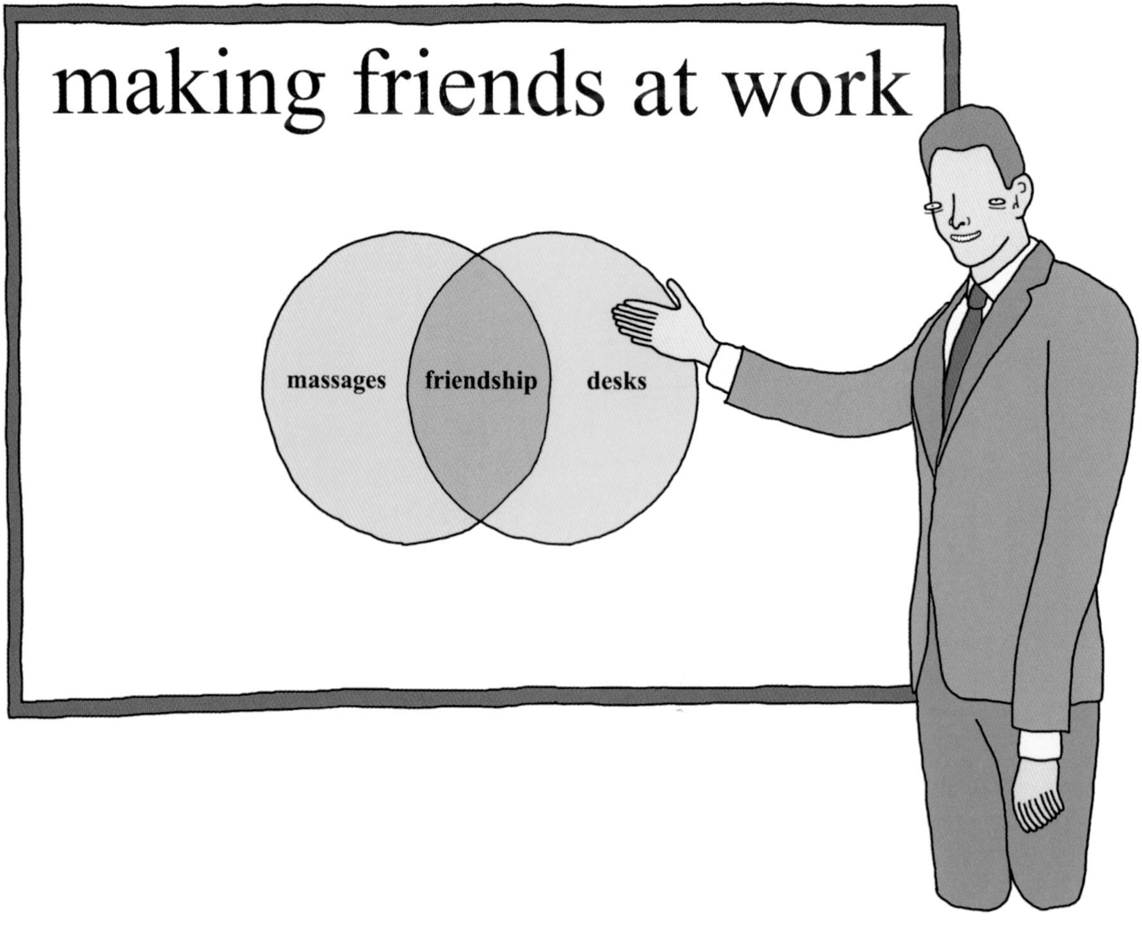
making friends at work
massages
friendship
desks

making friends with people at your work might sound rubbish
but it is actually a good thing to do and even though i have
never had a job in a office or a job at all apart from being a artist
and that time i had to polish the top of a
door at my mums work i have seen
people at work on my television
and in films before so i have quite
a good idea of how people make
friends at work so i hope that
in this section of my book i
will be able to help you to
make friends at your work
and build strong friendships
that will continue outside
of your work as well
good luck

i filled this
with my spit

nice

getting to know your colleagues

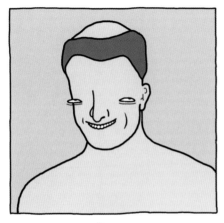

dean

- the cool guy
- gets all of the smiles
- knows riddles
- good at punching

klevin

- can see through brick
- good at doing words
- can taste electricity
- expert at computer

the 4 types of people at work

shona

- lives under her desk
- has 1 legs
- was in a malteaser advert
- calming eyes

venom

- cute and she knows it
- only drinks hens milk
- has no backs of her knees
- collects peoples thoughts

tell them about yourself

once you have found someone at your work that you want to be friends with it is a good idea for you to tell them a interesting fact about yourself to get them in a thirsty mood for your friendship

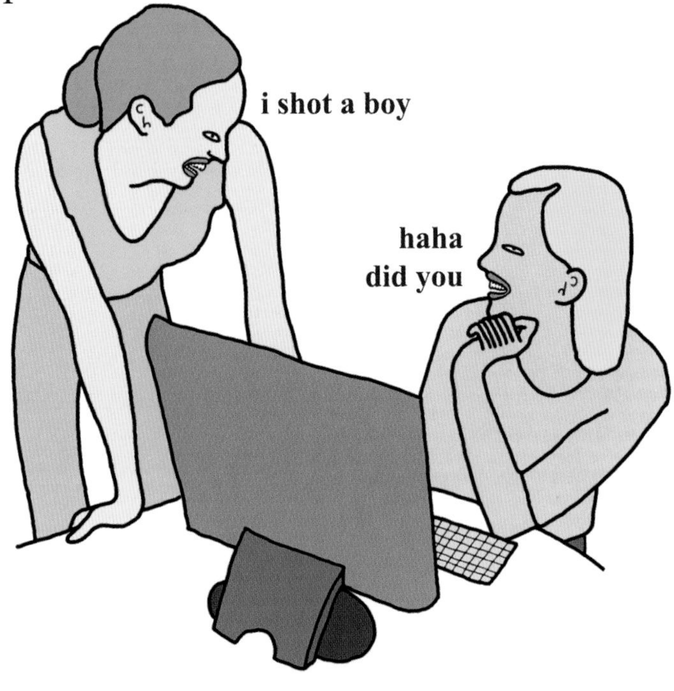
i shot a boy
haha
did you

bring food in to work

the way to a future friends heart is down their throat so you should bring the gift of some food into work for them to have a eat of so they will think you are a generous person and they will want to be friends with you

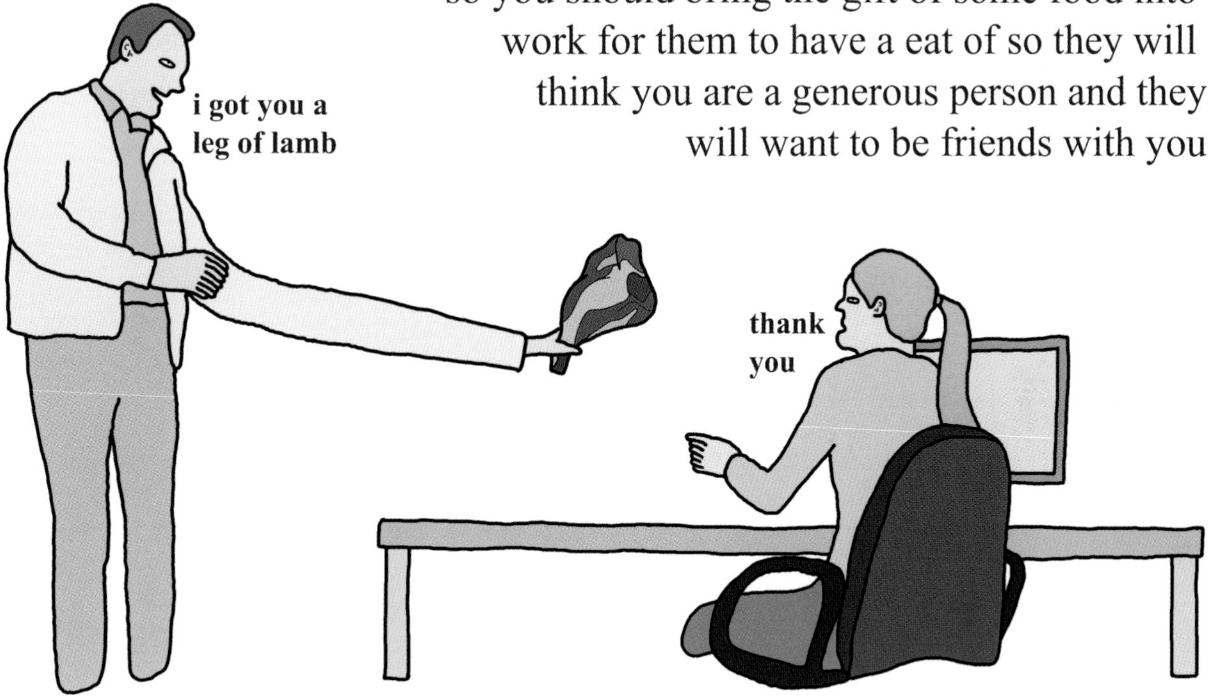
i got you a leg of lamb
thank you

give a surprise massage

a surprise massage is a great way to show someone at your work that you can be a sensual friend and you mean them no harm

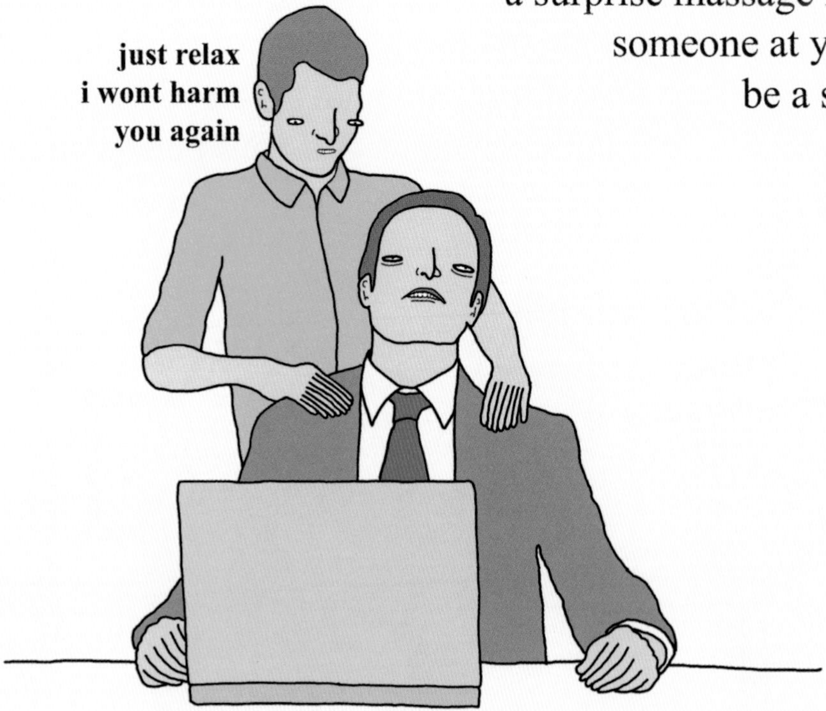
just relax
i wont harm
you again

making friends at a office party

a office party is a perfect place for you to make friends with someone at your work in a fun safe way

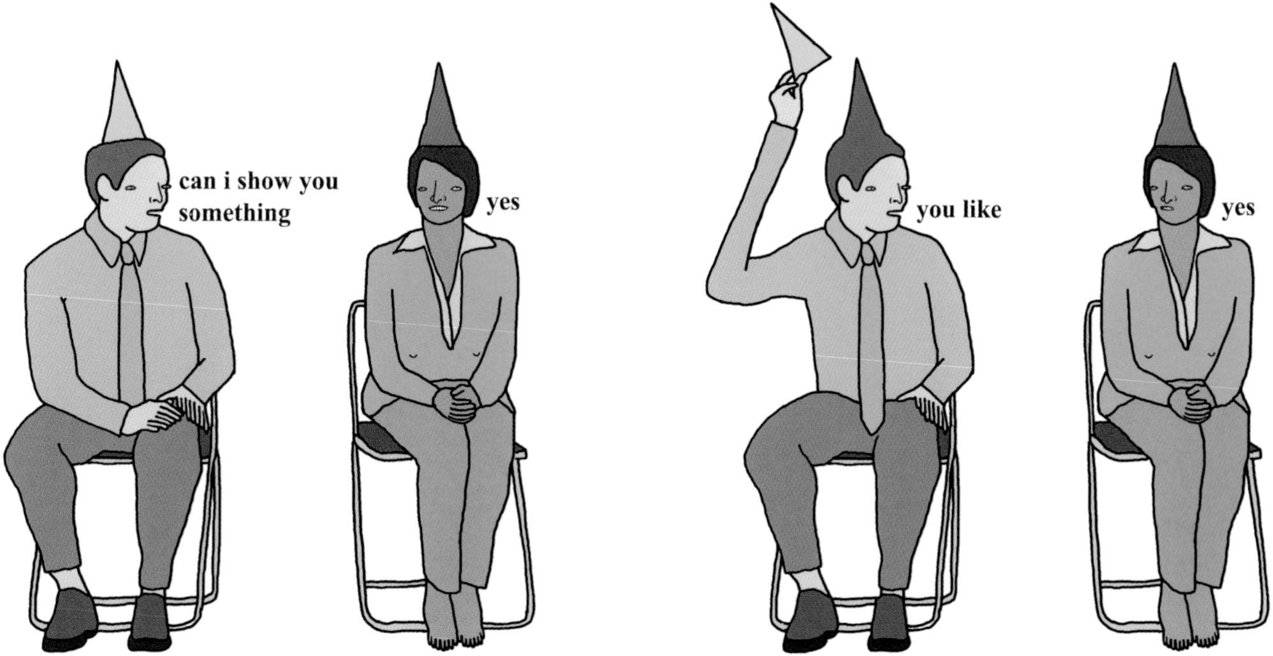
can i show you something
yes
you like
yes

this is fill and paul
they work in a office that sells knees
fill wants to be friends with paul
but fill is shy and he doesnt
know what to say to paul

paul

fill

question: what should fill say to paul to make him want to be his friend

a: it is really weather today
b: where is toilet
c: i am deaf

if you answered c i am deaf then you have chosen the correct answer because it is important to tell your future friend something fun and interesting about yourself so they will want to be your friend

after work drink

now that you have made a new friend at your work
why dont you ask them to go for a drink with
you after work so you can get to
know each other even more

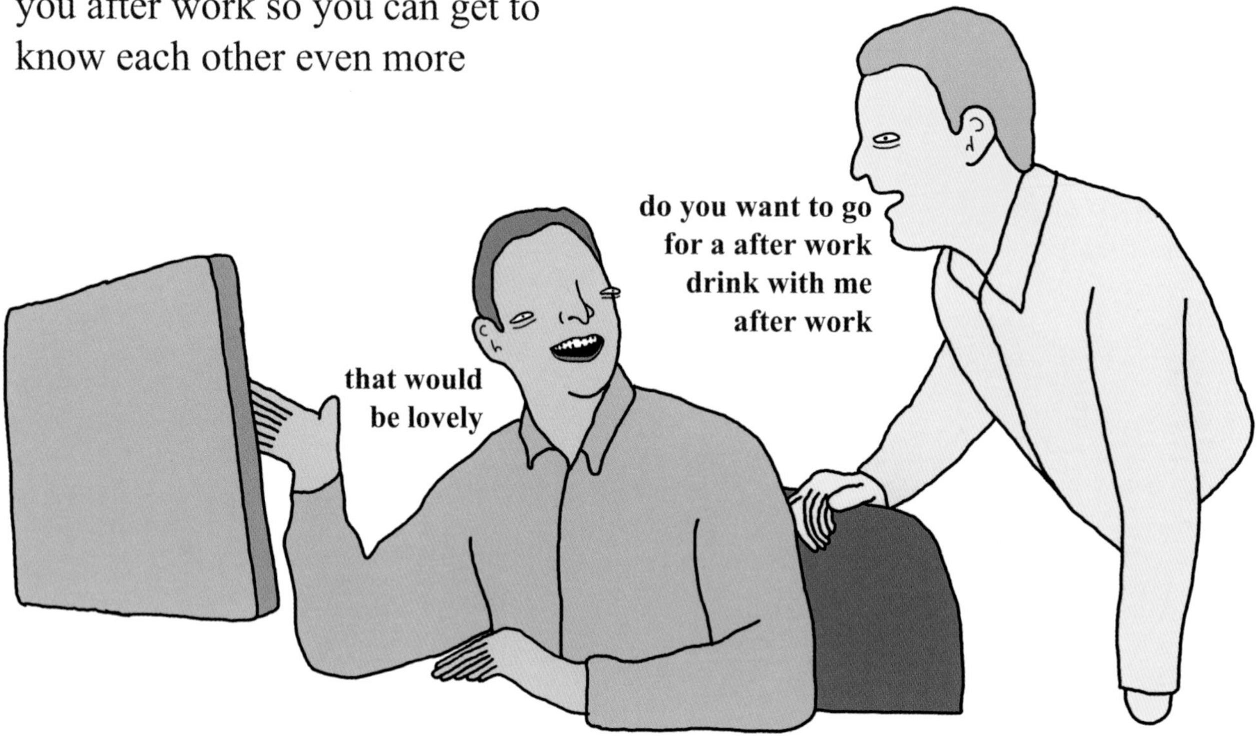
do you want to go
for a after work
drink with me
after work
that would
be lovely

a pond or a local lake is a good place for you
and your new work friend to have
a after work drink for yourselfs

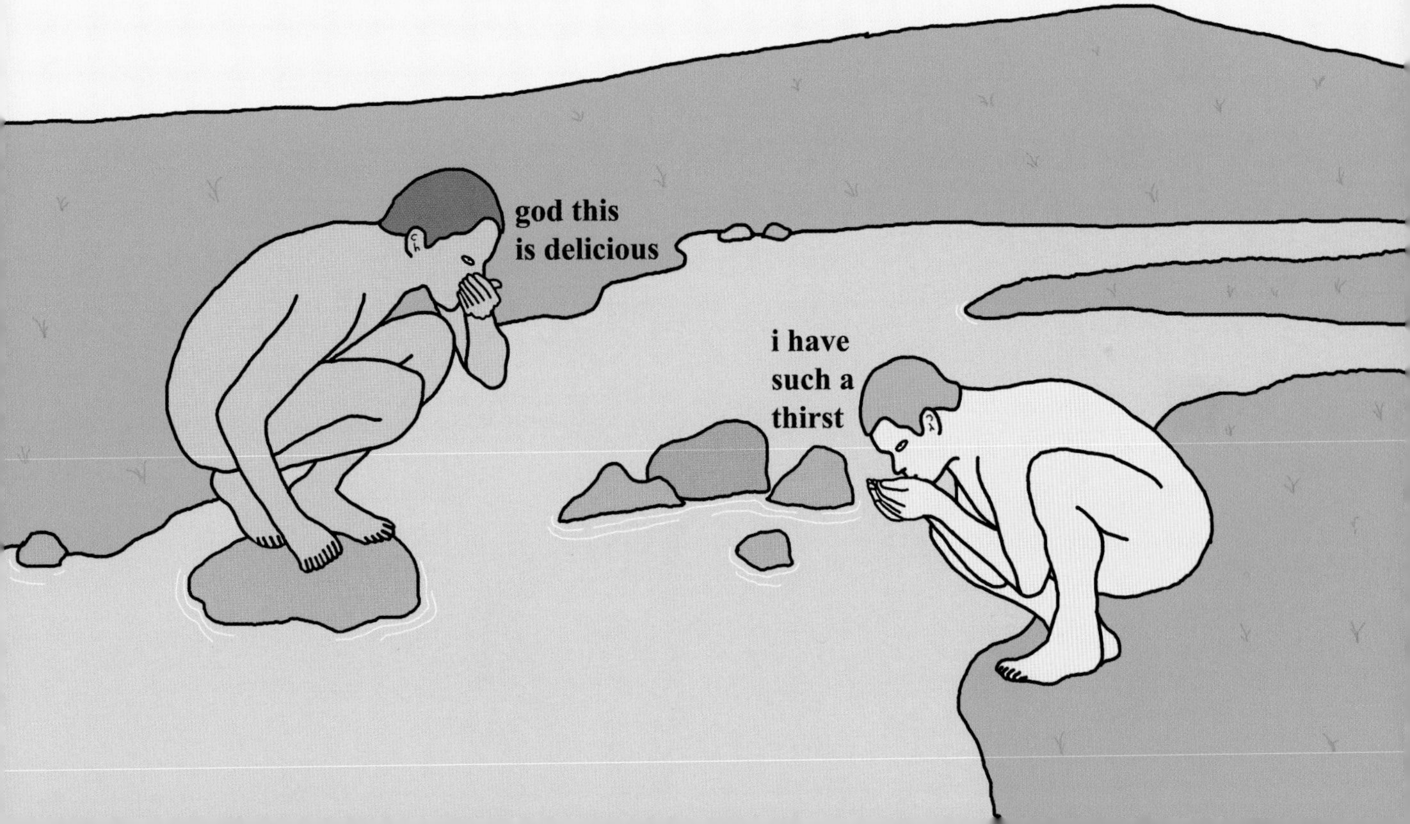
god this
is delicious
i have
such a
thirst

online friends

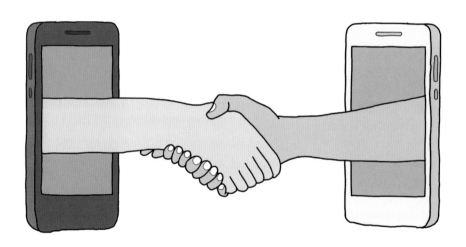

when you have a friend who lives inside of your phone or your computer
they are called a online friend
there is many different names for online friends like:

click cousins
pixel papas
keyboard

but most people just call internet friendship online friends
because it is a friend who is on the line

reasons why online friends are better than real life friends:
you can play games with them on the internet
they are always in your house

on the next few pages i will show you the best things that you can do
with your online friends on the internet

sharing videos

some of the most popular types of
videos that you can share with
your friends on the internet are:

i am birthed

a video of a mouse being born

a video of a colour blind boy being given special glasses that let him see the colour of blood for the very first time

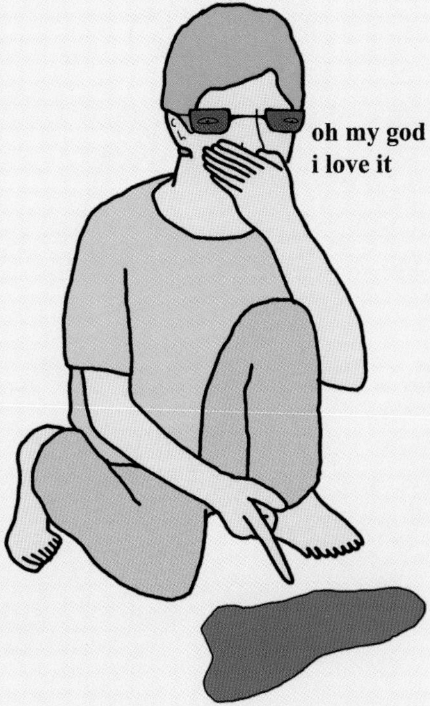
oh my god
i love it

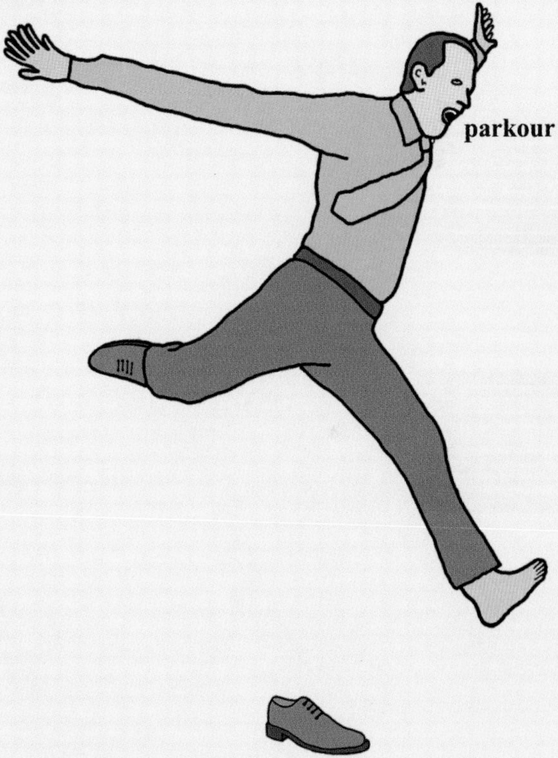
parkour

a video of a man jumping over a shoe

a great way to have fun with your friend on the internet is by playing online **games** the most popular online game in the world is called pass the crabs

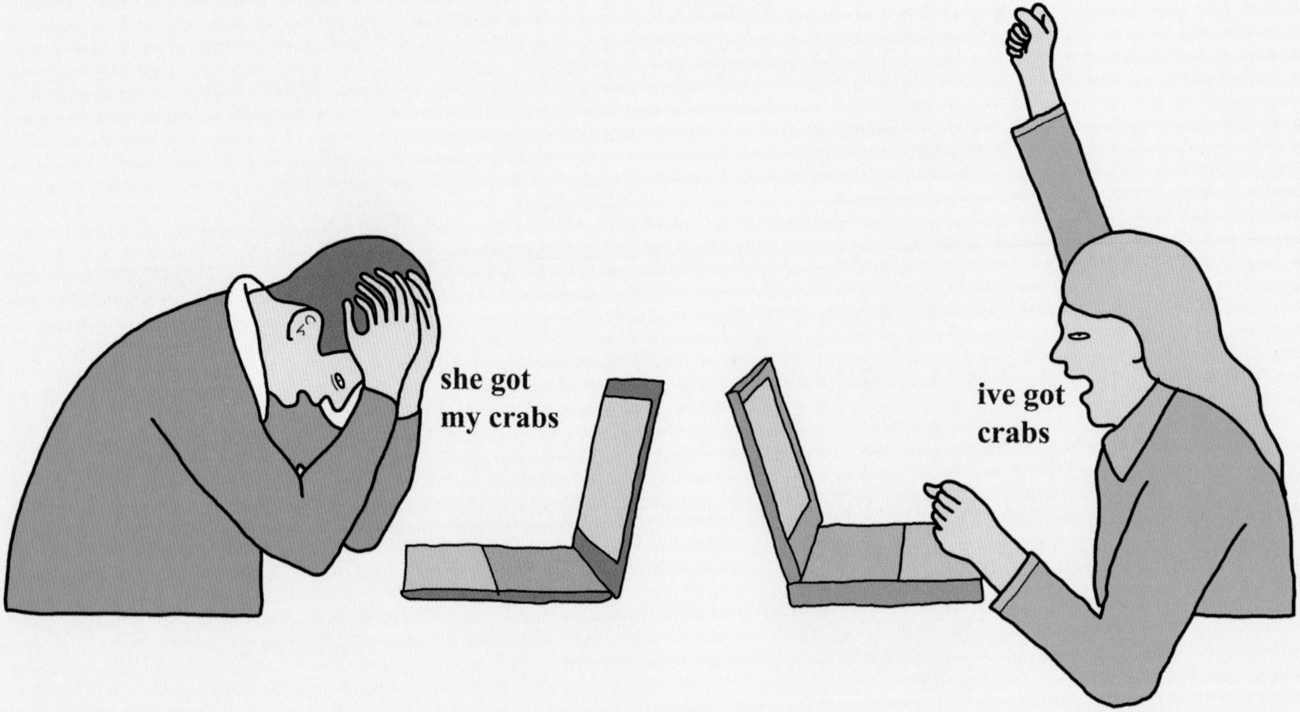
she got
my crabs
ive got
crabs

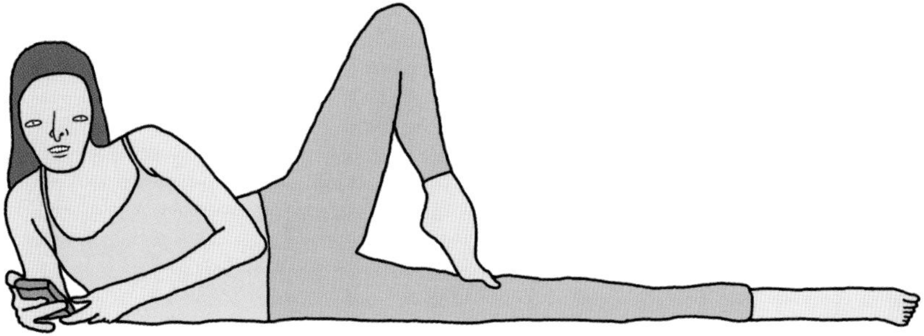

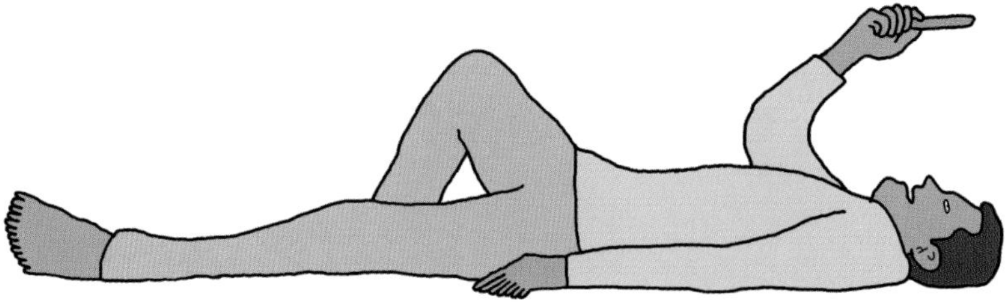

having a **chat** with your online friend on your phone or thightop computer is a good way to keep your friendship alive when you cant actually be in the same room as them to have a look at their voice coming out of their mouth

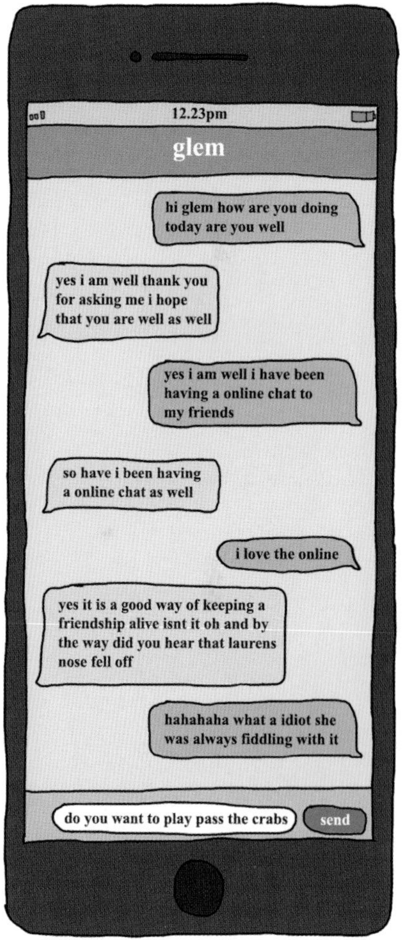
12.23pm
glem
hi glem how are you doing today are you well
yes i am well thank you for asking me i hope that you are well as well
yes i am well i have been having a online chat to my friends
so have i been having a online chat as well
i love the online
yes it is a good way of keeping a friendship alive isnt it oh and by the way did you hear that laurens nose fell off
hahahaha what a idiot she was always fiddling with it
do you want to play pass the crabs
send

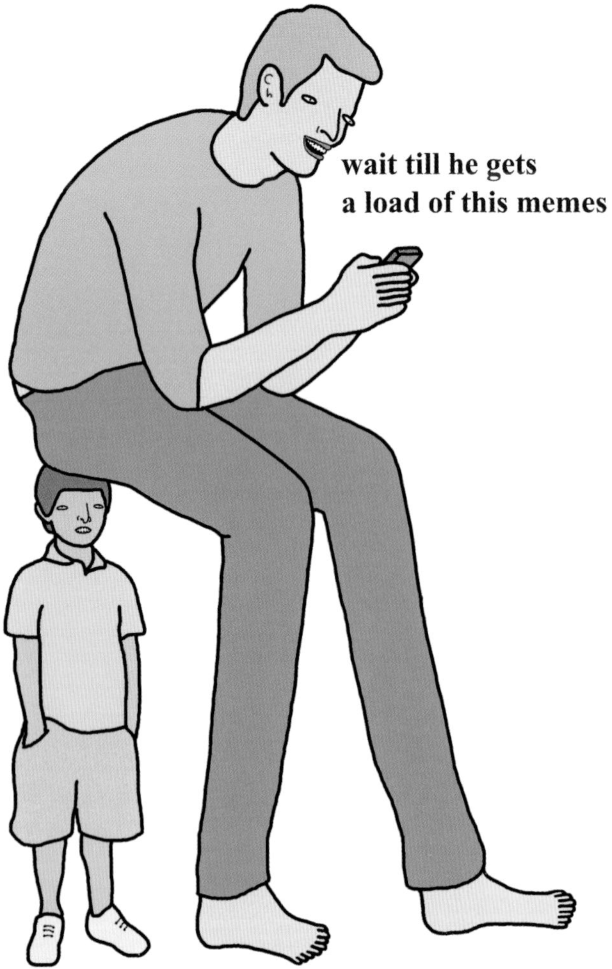
wait till he gets
a load of this memes

send each other memes

question: what is a memes

answer: a memes is a type of online picture about cats

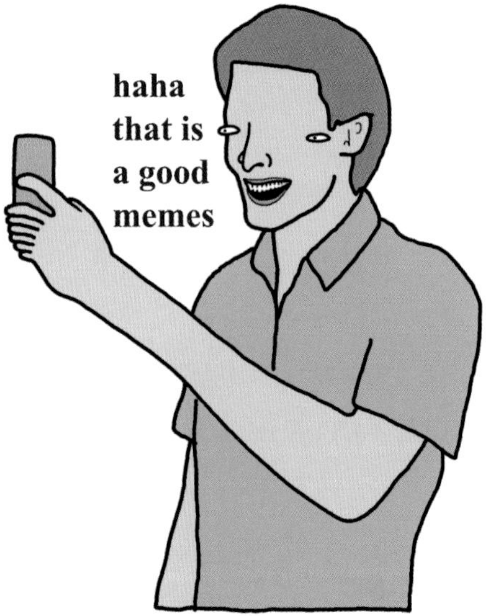
haha
that is
a good
memes

this is a memes

framily

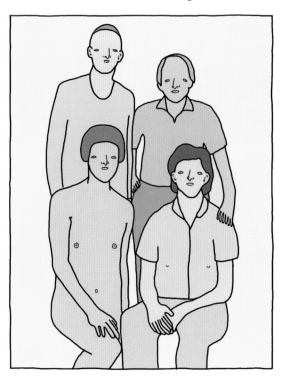

question: can you be friends with your family

answer: yes you can be friends with your family

when you are friends with someone who is in your family
they are called your framily

mothers

your mother is the first friend that you
will have in your life because she
let you live inside of her body
when you were little

thank
you for
letting
me live
inside
of you

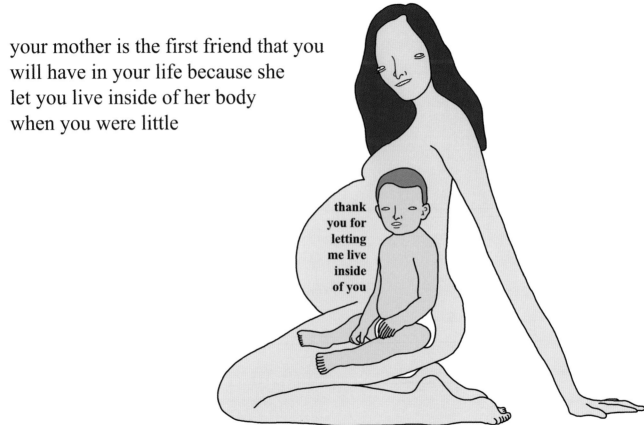

dads

if you want to be friends with your dad
it is important to find a activity that
you can both enjoy together
like shaving your backs

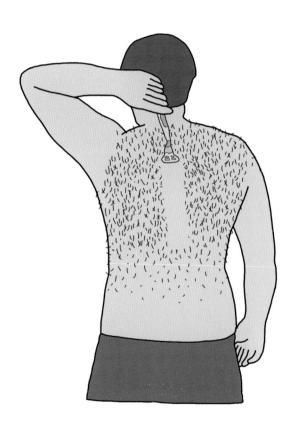
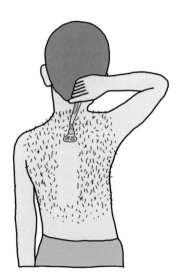

brothers

a brother is always there for you
when you need important
life advice

be honest
should i
dip it
yes
dip it
hehehehe

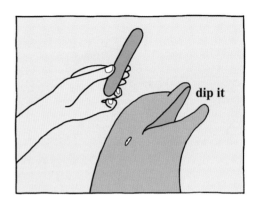

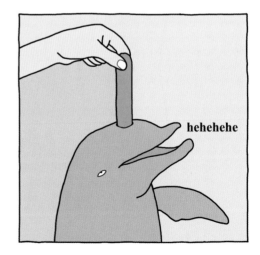

i love my sister
because her laugh
is as delicate as
two feathers
making love
in the rain

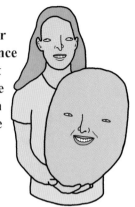

i love my sister
because she once
laid a egg that
looked like the
little boy from
the sixth sense

why i love my sister

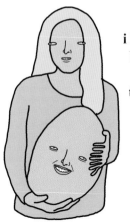

i love my sister
because she is
beautiful on
the inside and
that is all
that matters

i love my sister
because she looks
like a massive
swollen toe

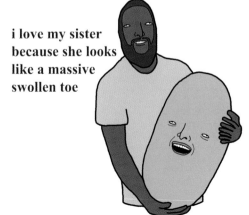

cousins

a cousin is your friend that is birthed from
your aunty or uncles womb to live
forever inside of your heart

cousin love

uncles

uncles make the best friends because they know the best jokes and they are good at stealing noses

got your sniff tip

my collection
is complete

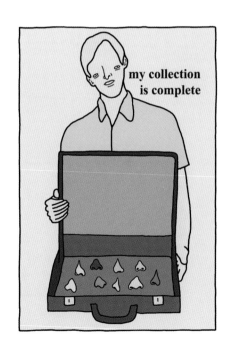

being friends
with animals

have you ever walked past a dog and thought
god i wish i could be friends with that guy
or have you ever seen a cat in your street
and imagined being its best friend
if your answer is yes then this chapter
of my book is for you because it is
all about being friends with animals

why animals make good friends

animals are better than people because they will never stab you
in the heart except for that one stingray that stabbed steve irwin
in his heart but apart from that idiot (the stingray not steve irwin)
animals are friendly people who have nothing but love to give
and that is why they make perfect friends

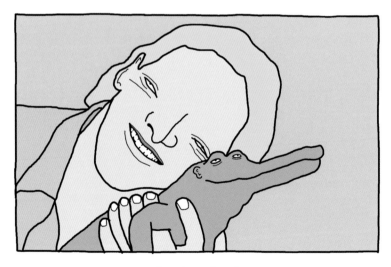

rip steve irwin

the sunshine doesnt
come from the skies
it comes from the love
thats inside a dogs eyes

the types of animals that make the best friends

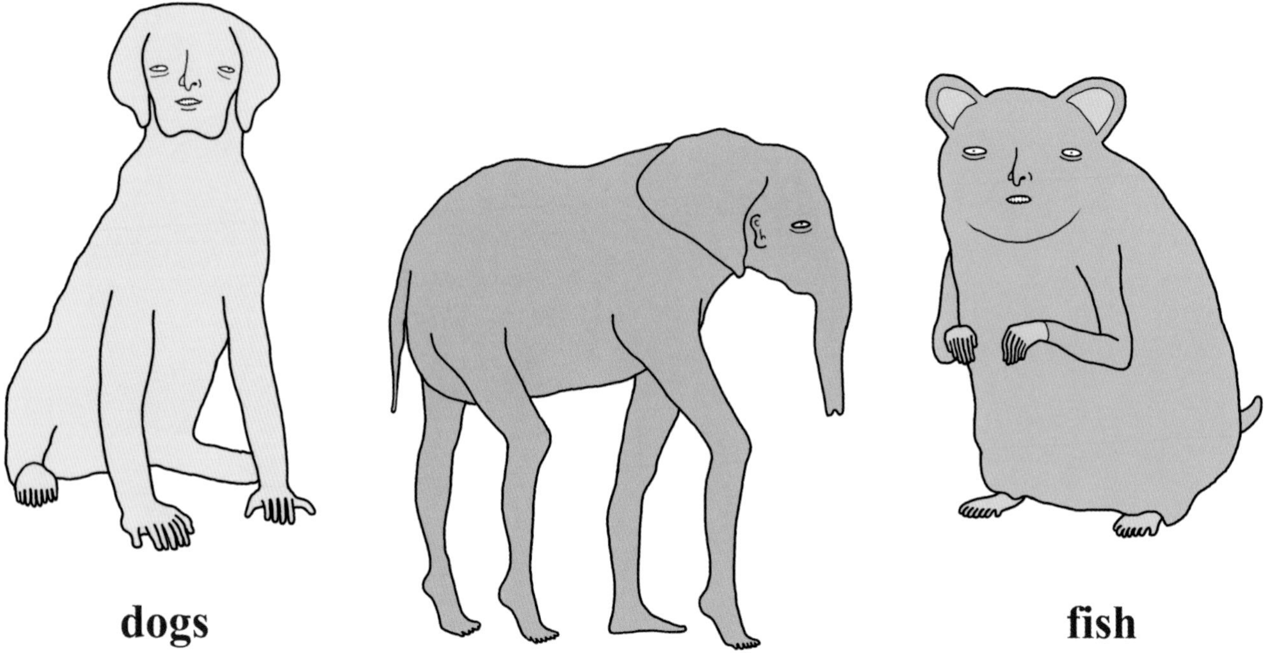

dogs

grey angels

fish

more types of animals that make the best friends

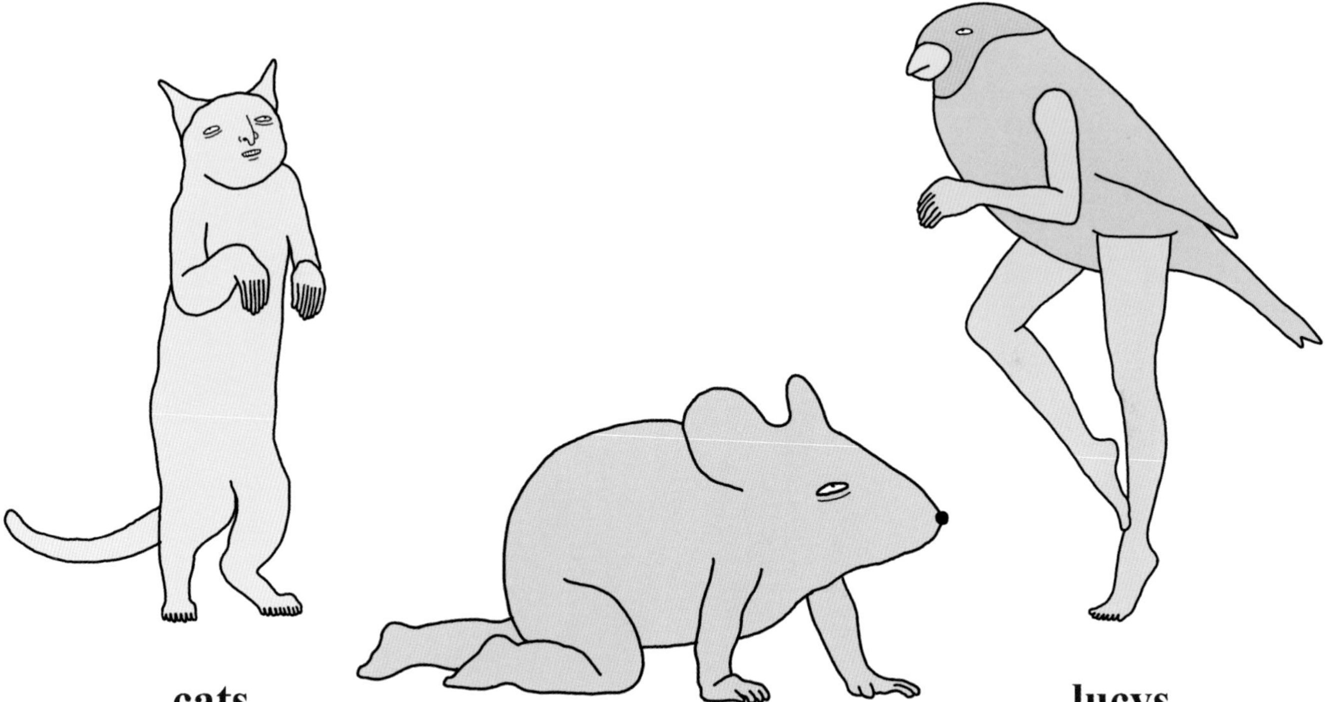

cats

little richards

lucys

animals are good listeners

dogs are the best
listeners and the
greatest keeper
of secrets

whispering
i wont tell
a single soul

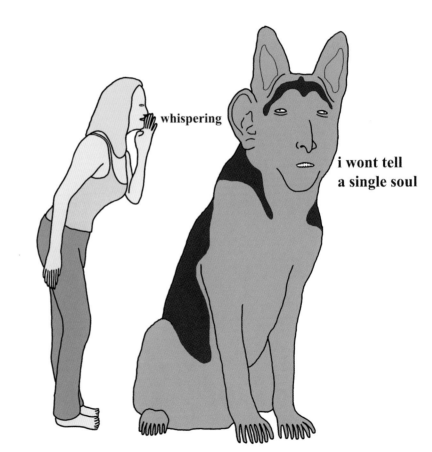

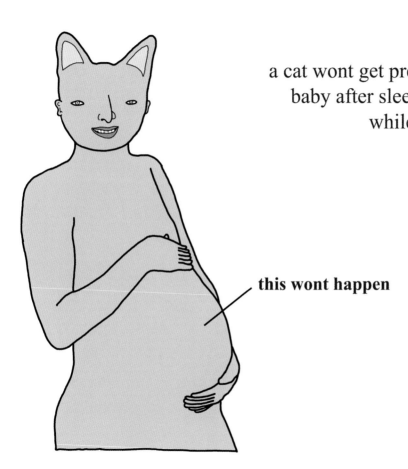

animals are faithful

a cat wont get pregnant with your boyfriends
baby after sleeping with him in the garden
while you were at work and then
act like it isnt his baby for
half a year even when
you knew fine well it
was his baby because
it has got the same
eyeballs as him

this wont happen

animals are good for your health

walking your animal friend is a good way to keep yourself healthy
and to meet other healthy hearted humans who arent going
to die soon from heart failure

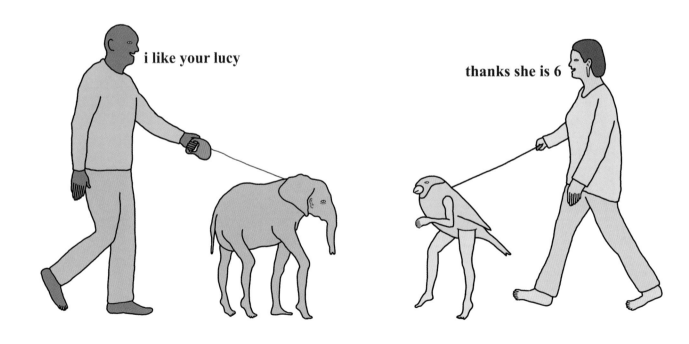

i like your lucy

thanks she is 6

try it yourself

a fun quick 13 minute task
for you to do is to lie down
and close your eyes and
imagine that you are your
favourite animal
how does this make you feel
circle **yes** or **no**

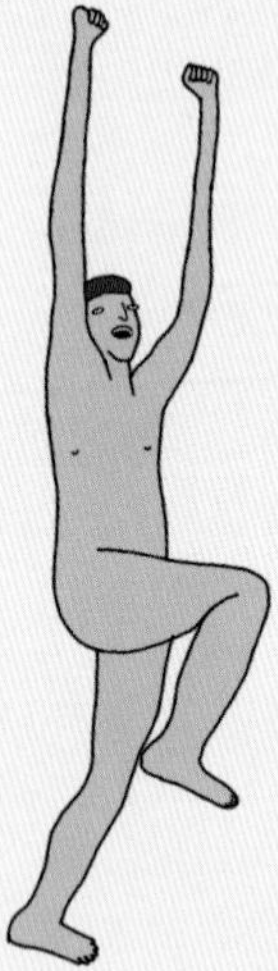

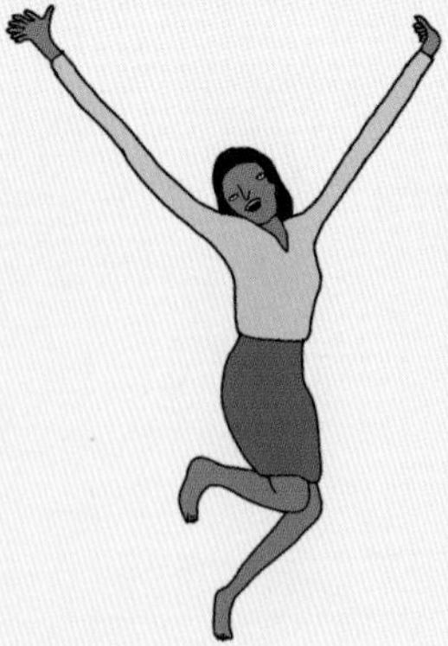

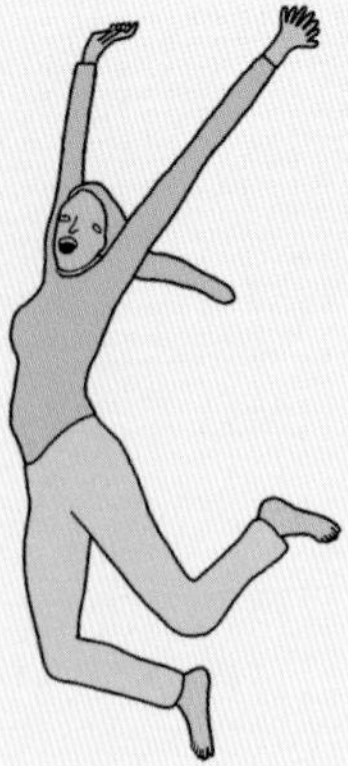

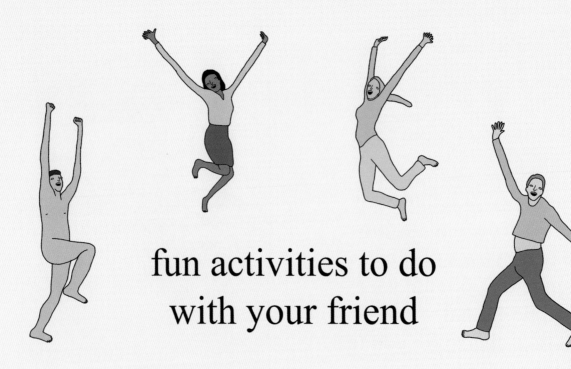

fun activities to do with your friend

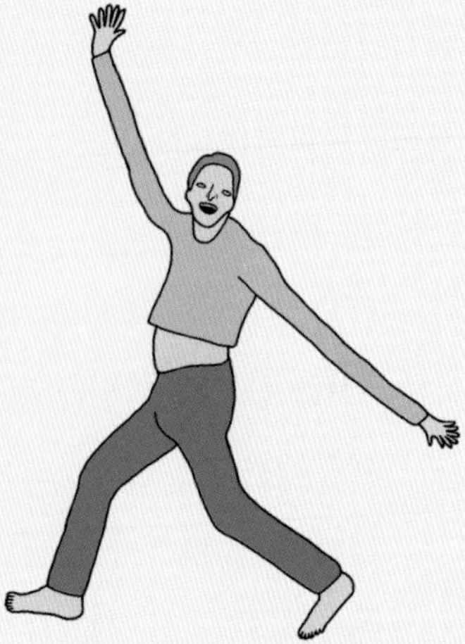

i am having fun

i am also having fun

now that you have a friend
it is important that you do
some fun things with them
so they dont get bored of you
and you can keep your
beautiful friendship alive

listen to the inside of your friends body

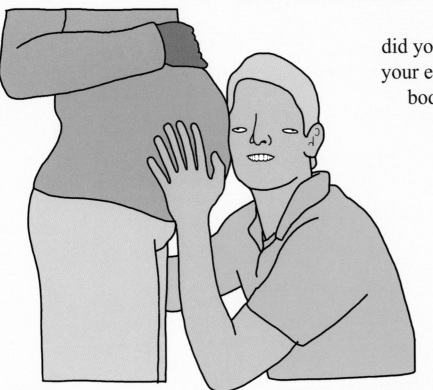

did you know that if you put
your ear next to your friends
body you can hear lots of
different sounds

this man can hear the
sound of a fisherman
who is lost at sea

why dont you try
it out on your
own friend

other sounds you can hear inside of your friends body:

i can hear
mice

i can hear
andrew lloyd webber

i can hear
a screaming boy

visit a old person

on the outside old people might look like rotten sacks of death
but if you actually get to know them you will find out
that on the inside they are actually quite
interesting and spending a hour
talking to them is a fun thing
for you and your friend
to do together

try it yourself

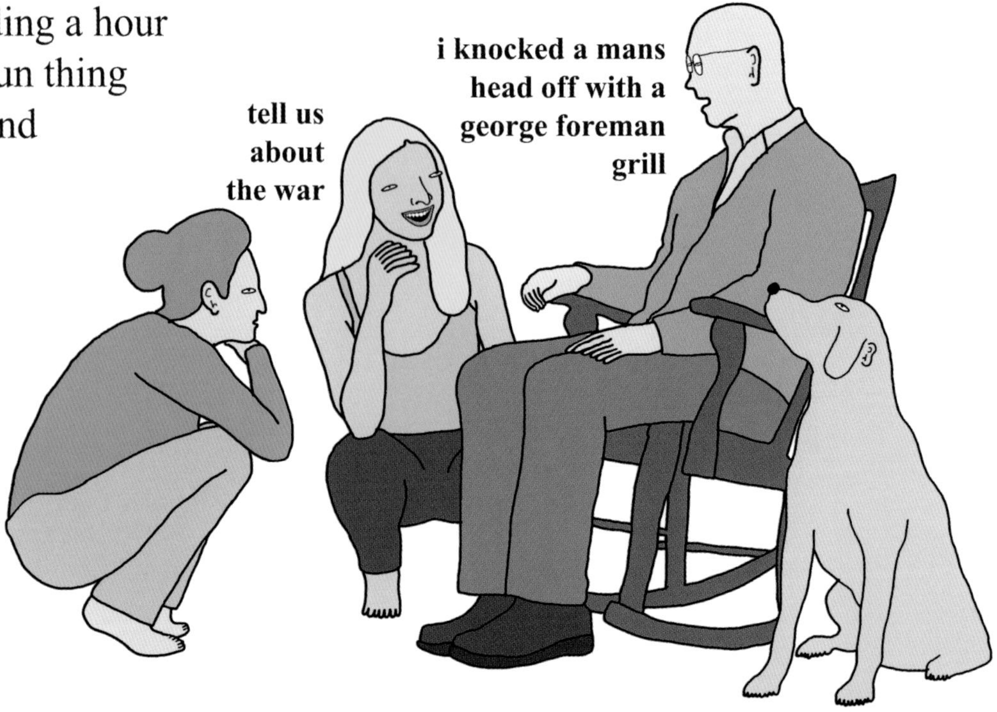
tell us about the war
i knocked a mans head off with a george foreman grill

a day out at a local
petting farm is a fun
way to spend a day

visit a local petting farm

get petted by your favourite
animals while spending
a quality of time with
your friend

rolling down a hill

nothing says friendship more than the feeling of rolling
down a hill with your best friend on a beautiful warming day

this lady who looks like a massive swollen toe is called loraine but everyone calls her t bone for short and i always see her rolling down the big hill that is near my house and she is always so happy and laughing her head off and she lets the local children take turns to carry her up to the top of the hill and then roll her down it again and sometimes when i am having a panic attack i like to sit at the top of the hill and watch t bone rolling down because the happiness that she brings to all of the children makes me not feel like i am going to die anymore and one time i thanked her and she said what for and then i said for the happiness that you bring and then she said i just like rolling down the hill and i said you are good at it and she said i know and then she said watch this and she rolled herself down the hill so fast that she knocked over a old man who was walking his dog and me and t bone and the old man just burst out laughing and even though the old man died on his way to the hospital it was still really lovely that we all got to laugh together in his final moments because it is better to die with your friends surrounded by laughter than to just die in your house on your own surrounded by tins of old soup and torn out magazine pictures of martin clunes

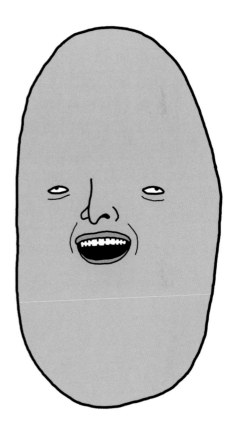

milk a friend

drinking your friends milk is a fun and personal way of bonding
it is also a good source of protein and calcium
which builds healthy bones and teeth
so you can build up the strength
to be a better friend

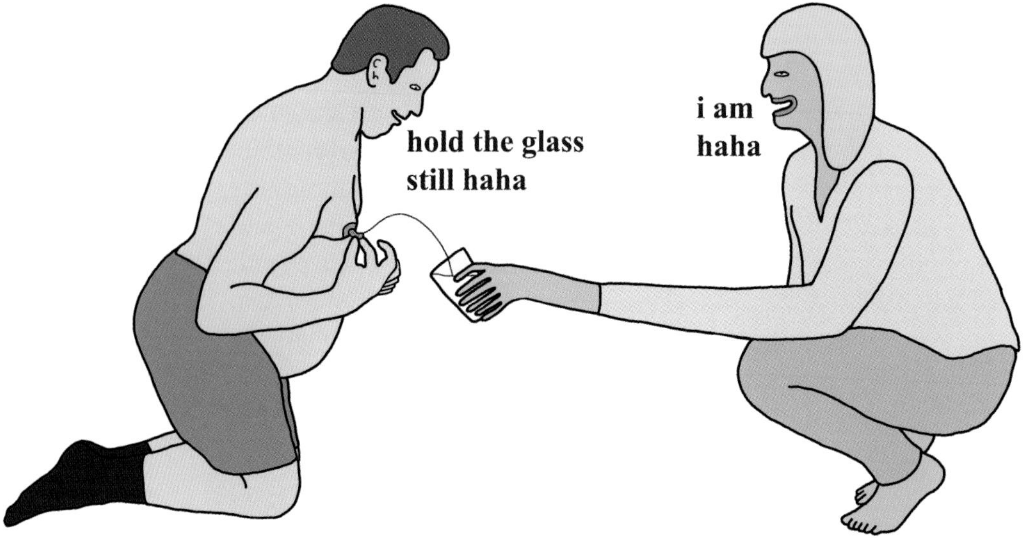
hold the glass still haha
i am haha

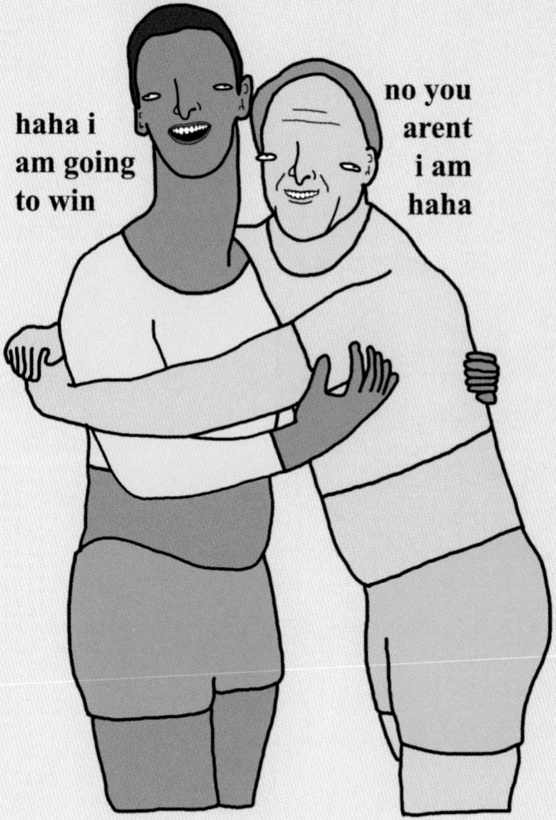
haha i am going to win
no you arent i am haha

have a cuddling competition

if you and your friend are quite competitive then why not have a cuddling competition to find out who is the best at cuddling for once and for all

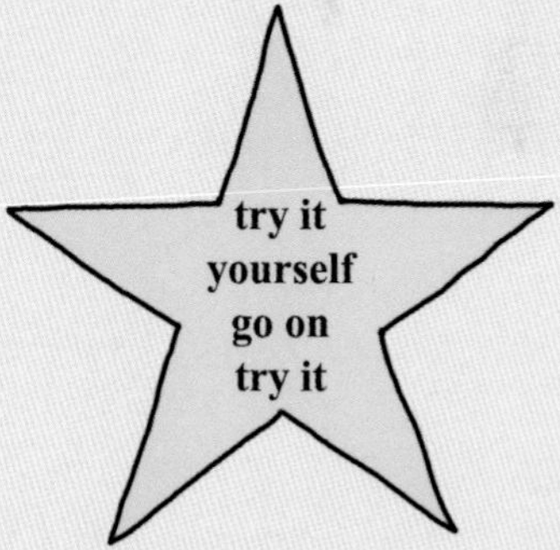
try it yourself go on try it

white eyes

why not spend a afternoon making
your eyes go completely white with your friend

the little boy in my picture is called darren but everyone calls him the depth of a thousand seas for short because he can make his eyes go completely white like he has swam to the bottom of the sea and his eyes have gone completely white because he has no use for them anymore because it is so dark that far under the sea and i saw a documentary about him on my television before and the man who was having a interview of him kept on asking darren to make his eyes go completely white but darren kept on saying he didnt want to do it but every time the man looked away darren would look at the camera and make his eyes go completely white really quickly and the man kept on saying did you just make your eyes turn completely white when i looked away there and darren kept on going no i dont think so and the man said good because i want to see them when you do it and darren kept on saying yeah i know and then when the man looked away again darren made his eyes go completely white and the man looked at him really quickly and he said i could have sworn i saw your eyes go completely white just then and darren said nope i think you are imaging it and he was trying not to burst out laughing and then right at the end of the documentary it showed darren and the man sitting in the mans car and the man said right darren before i drop you off at your house are you going to give me a glimpse of those famous white eyes of yours and darren said ok then and he went right up to the mans face and he put his eyes right next to the mans eyes and he made his eyes go completely white and the man said now thats what you call a couple of completely white eyes and then darren said see ya in a really deep slow motion voice and then it showed him walking up his driveway back to his house in slow motion and the song that is called one day like this by the pop group elbow started playing and it was probably one of the best documentary programmes that i have ever seen in my whole life i hope that it wins all of the awards

cheering up your friend

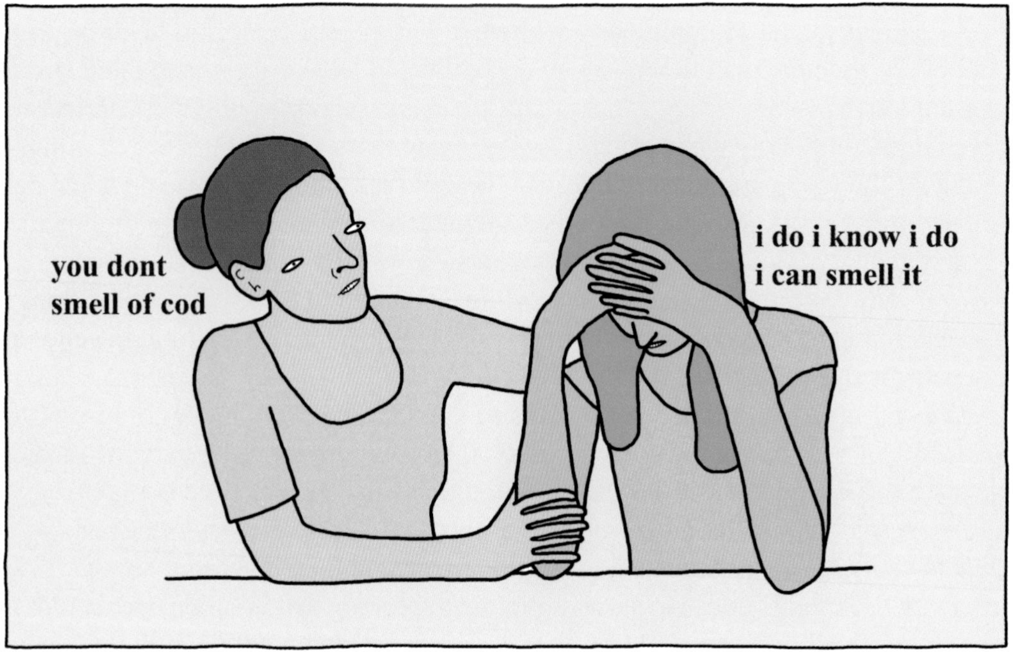
you dont
smell of cod
i do i know i do
i can smell it

if your friend one day becomes quiet or doesnt want to do anything then it probably means that they are depressed

question:
what is depressed

answer:
good question when a person is depressed it means that they find emptiness in life and it is your job as a friend to fill their life with things that give it meaning

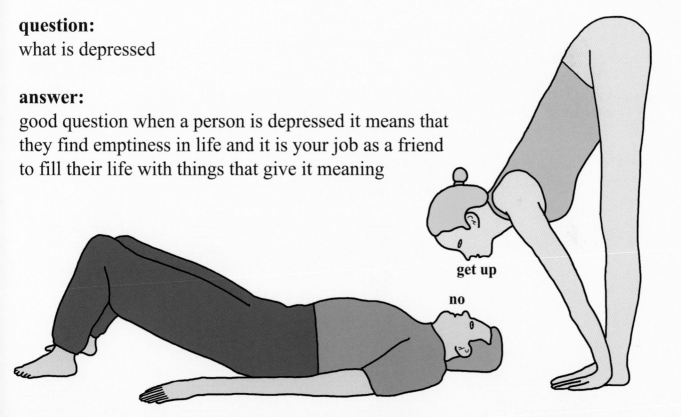

get up

no

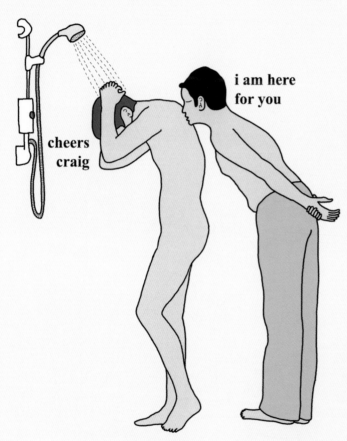

cheers
craig

i am here
for you

a thoughtful thing that you can do if
you think your friend is having a bad
day for themself is to run them a
shower to help them relax

extra tip:
why not gently kiss your friends back
while they shower to let them know
that you are there for them if they
want to talk to you

how to cheer up a miserable friend:

hide inside your friends toothpaste tube
to give them a mysterious minty fresh surprise

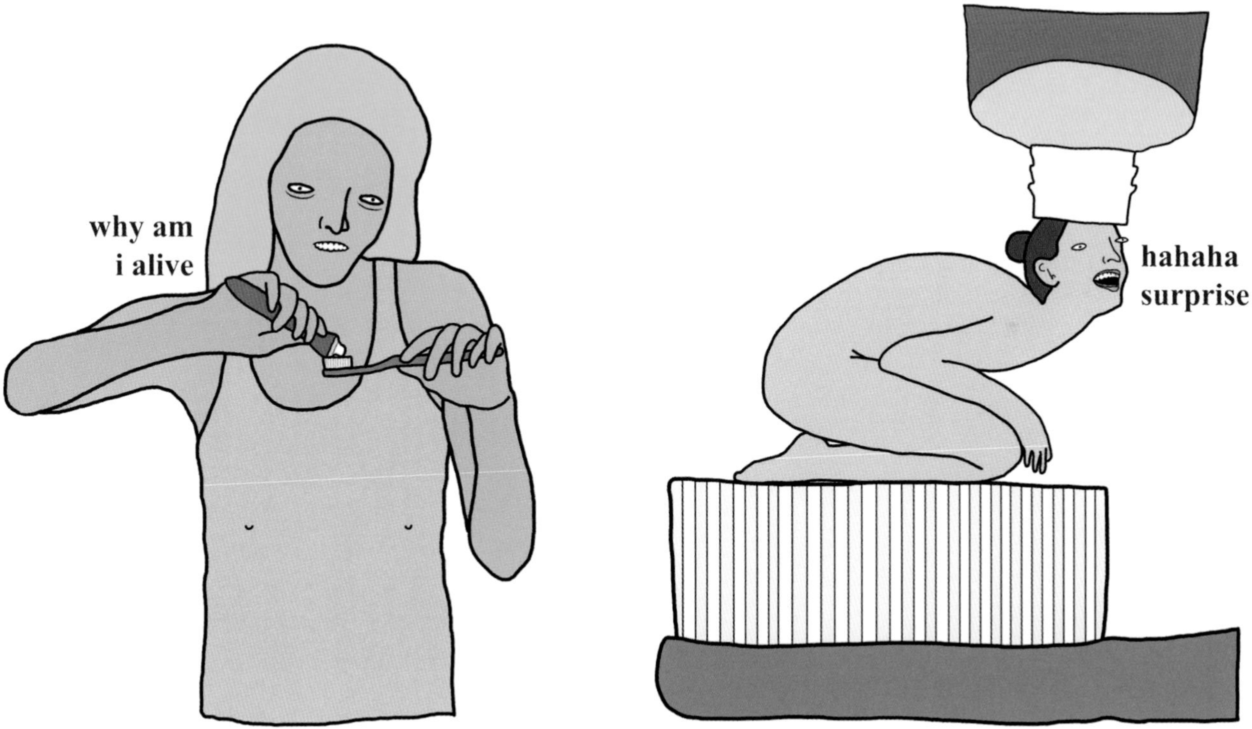
why am
i alive
hahaha
surprise

give them hope

if your friend is lonely then why
not buy them a cat to give them
some hope that they will not
die alone

no more
lonely

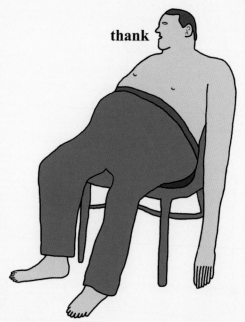

thank

i love my cat
because he eats
the mice so i
dont have to
anymore

i love my cat
because he
doesnt mind
that i smell
of fish

why i love my cat

i love my cat
because his
warming smile
takes away
the pain of life

i love my cat
because she
ate my son
so now she is
my son

the healing power of food

cooking a delicious meal for your friend
is a thoughtful way for you to
heal their broken heart

eat with your friend

dont eat your friend

tickle time

the most easiest way to cheer up your friend
is by having a tickle of them

when a person is tickled it releases
a chemical in their throat that
makes their voice turn
into laughter

laughter is the oppisite
of wanting to die

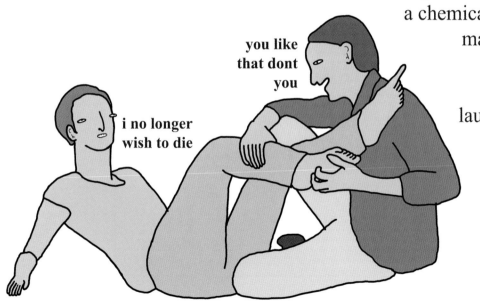

you like
that dont
you

i no longer
wish to die

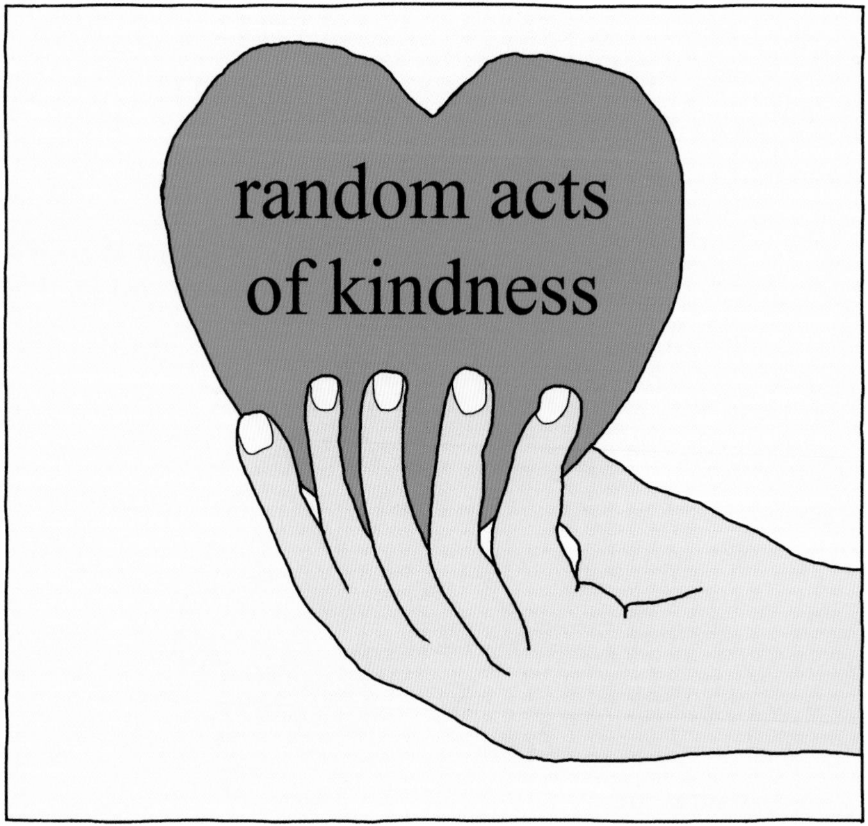
random acts
of kindness

a random act of kindness can lift the mood of a stranger
or a friend and help them feel glad to be alive
just think how beautiful the world would be if
everyone did one thing every day to make
someone else feel happy

so in this part of my book i will show you some
simple acts of kindess that you can do
to make your friends and strangers smile

random act of kindness:

softly kiss the postmans fingers when he puts them through your door to let him know that you are thankful for his gifts

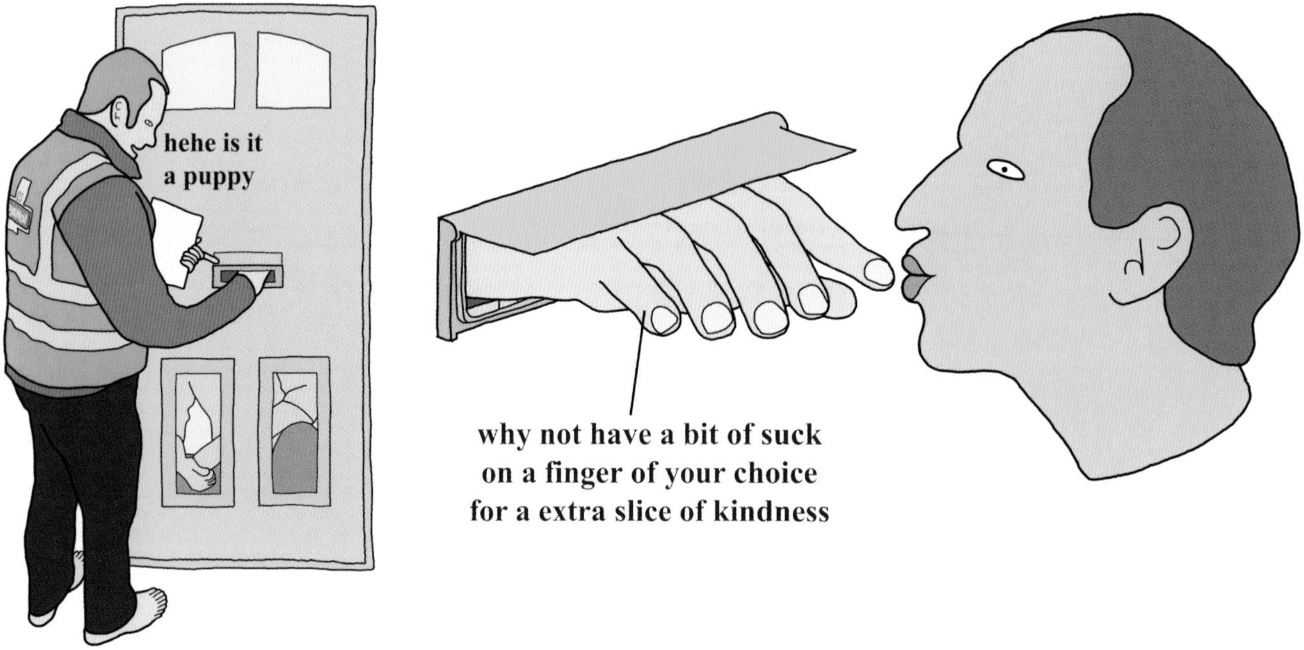
hehe is it
a puppy
why not have a bit of suck
on a finger of your choice
for a extra slice of kindness

the postmans name is called callum and he is my best postman of my whole life and every single morning when he comes to my door he always says wheres my puppy and he puts his hand through my letterbox and i always do such light kisses on his fingers to thank him for his gifts and one time when i was having a bit of a suck on his main finger it was so relaxing for me that i fell asleep and when i woke up 4 hours later i still had callums finger inside of my mouth and when i took it out of my mouth it was so small and floppy and white and me and callum just burst out laughing and he kept on shaking his hand to make it flop about and we couldnt stop laughing and i nearly even had a panic attack because i was laughing so much and sometimes to this very day when i am feeling dead sad i like to have a think about callums small white floppy finger and it always makes me glad to be alive and i am thankful for his friendship

friendship wig

give a friend a friendship wig made out of your own hair
so they can always be reminded of you
when they have a wear of it

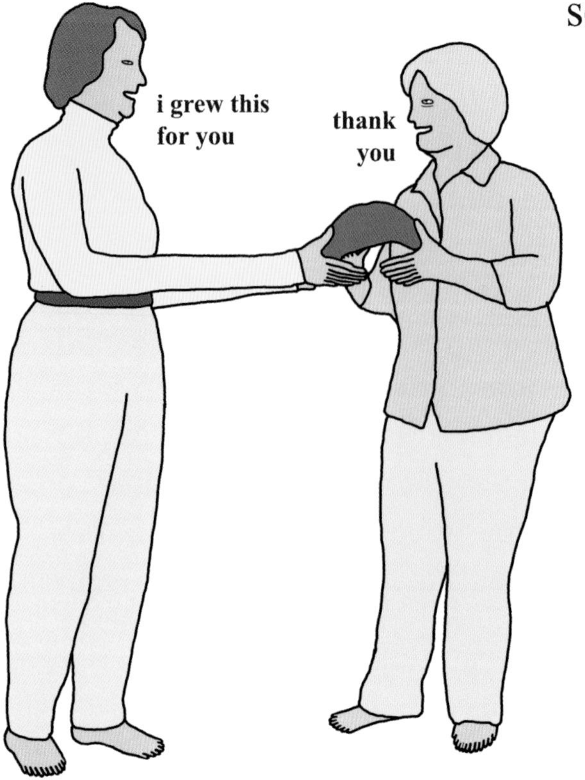
i grew this
for you
thank
you

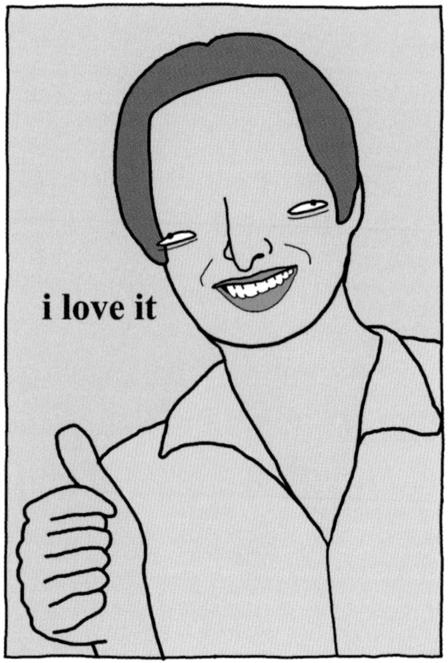
i love it

yum mayonnaise
my favourite
no problemo

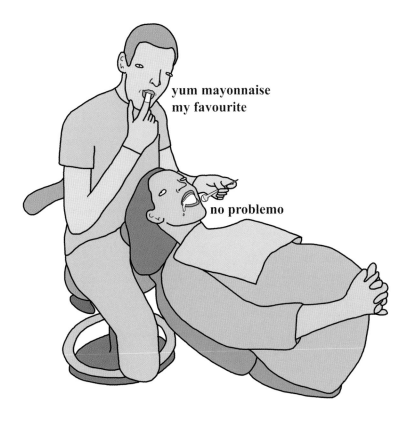

when you are at the dentist fill your mouth up with mayonnaise so the dentist can have a snack on it while he is checking your teeth dress up as the ghost of a old mans wife to share one final kiss with him to make him smile again

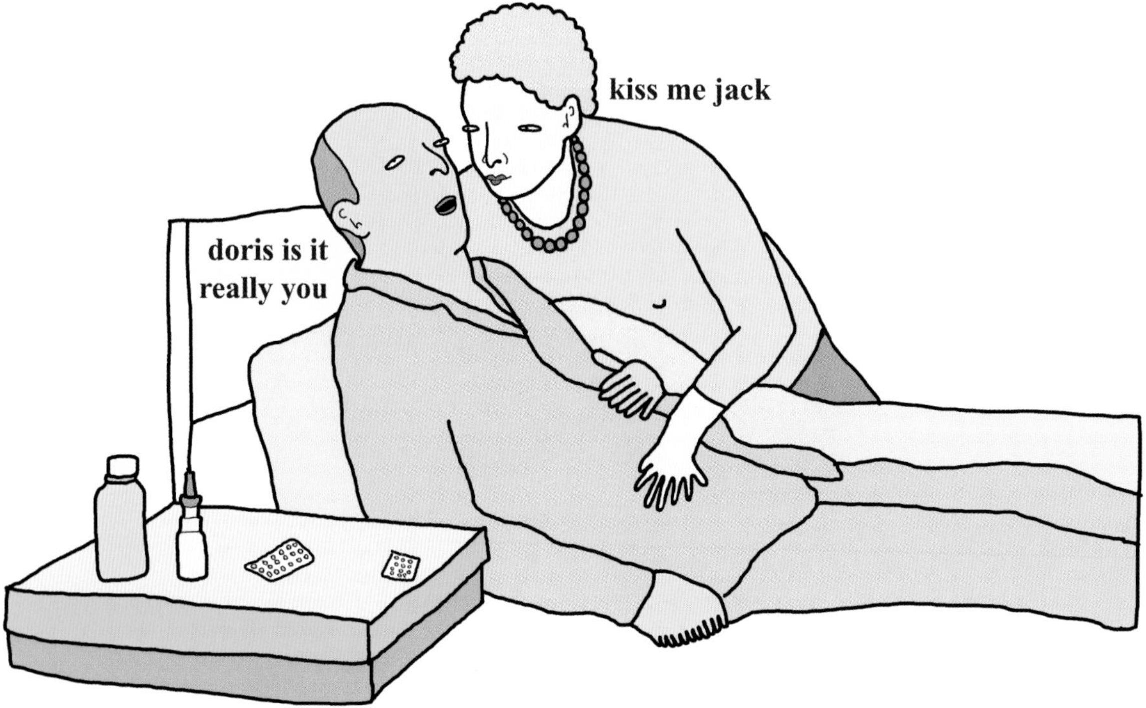
kiss me jack
doris is it really you

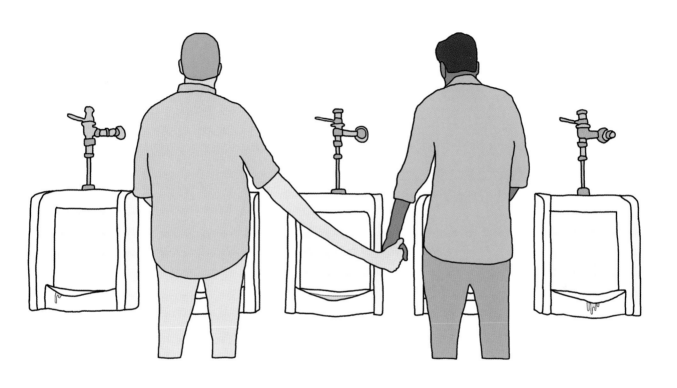

when you are next to someone at a urinal
reach out and hold their hand to make them feel less nervous

paint her nails

paint your friends nails for her
while she sleeps to give her
a nice surprise when
she wakes up

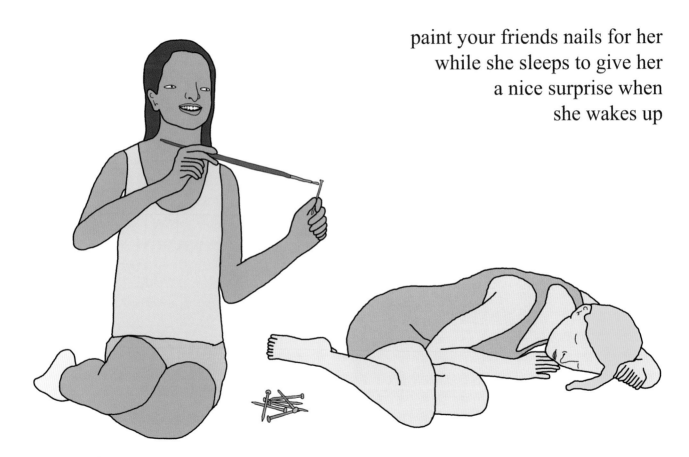

random act of kindness:

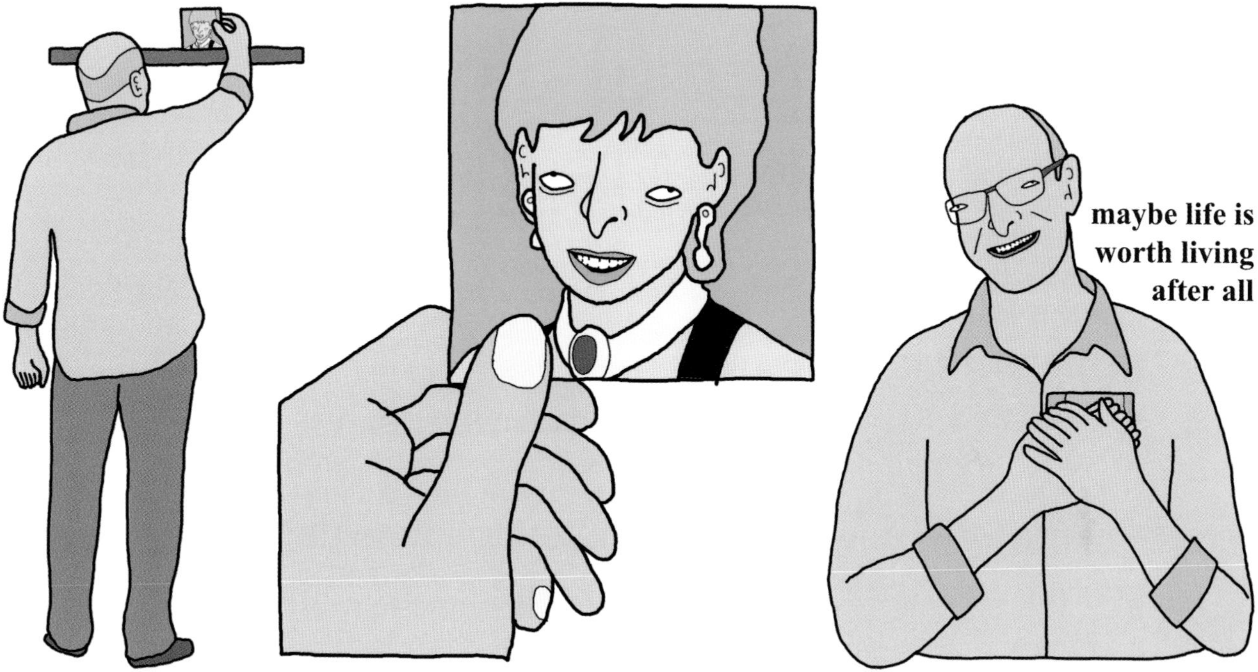
maybe life is
worth living
after all

leave a picture of princess diana on a shelf
to make someone feel glad to be alive

special days
and celebrations

being there for your friend on a special day in their life is
such a important part of friendship

over the next few pages i will help you to know the most important
special days of your friends life and give you some ideas of how
to have a celebrate of these special days with your friend
so you can be the most caring friend in town

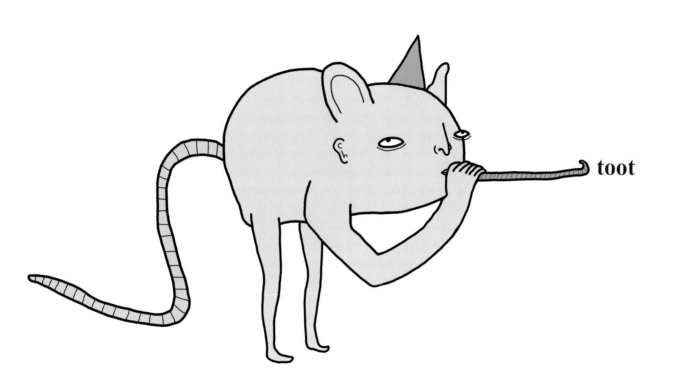

toot

birthdays

did you know that in a persons lifetime they
will celebrate more than 35 birthdays
wow that is a lot of births isnt it

a nice thing to do for a
friend on their birthday
is to give them a fun
birthday surprise

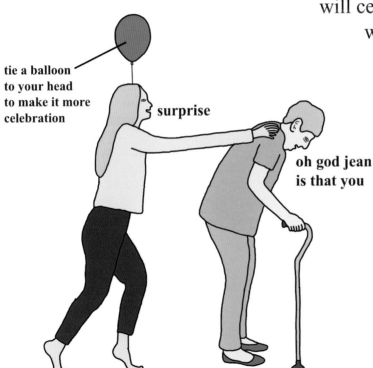

tie a balloon
to your head
to make it more
celebration

surprise

oh god jean
is that you

christmas

at christmas time a fun game you can play with your friend
is called secret santa

how to play: you and your friend both take turns to whisper a secret
inside of santas ear and the person who whispers the most secrets
in 1 hour gets to lick the sugar off santas fingers

 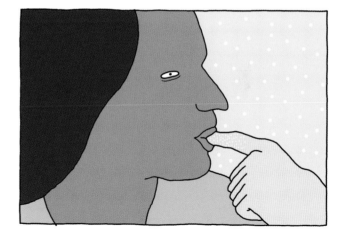

weddings

when your best friend gets married they will ask you to be their best man
a best man has to do a talk at the wedding that is called a speeching
say something funny about your friend in the speeching

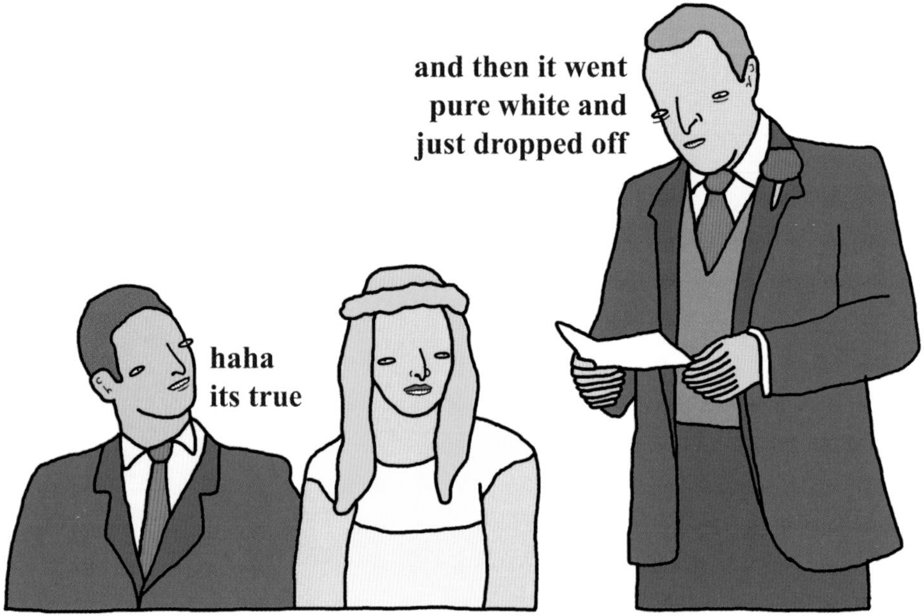
and then it went pure white and just dropped off
haha its true

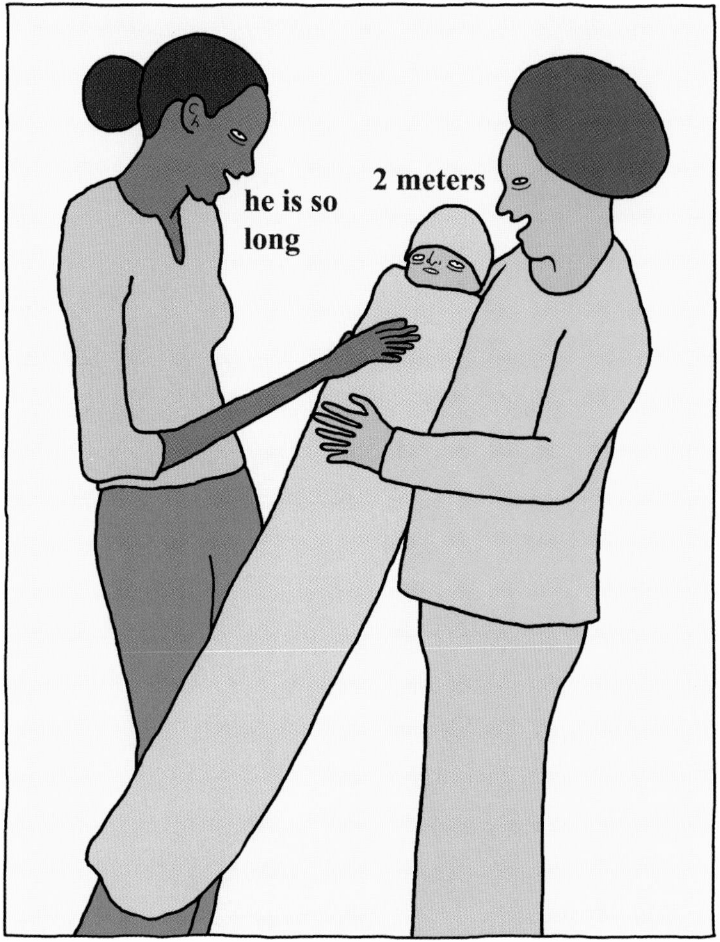
he is so
long
2 meters

the birth of a child

if your friend births a baby out of her you will have to meet the baby for the first time

it is important to compliment the baby to make your friend feel like she has made the right decision

new job

when your friend gets a new job you should give them a new job plum to say well done

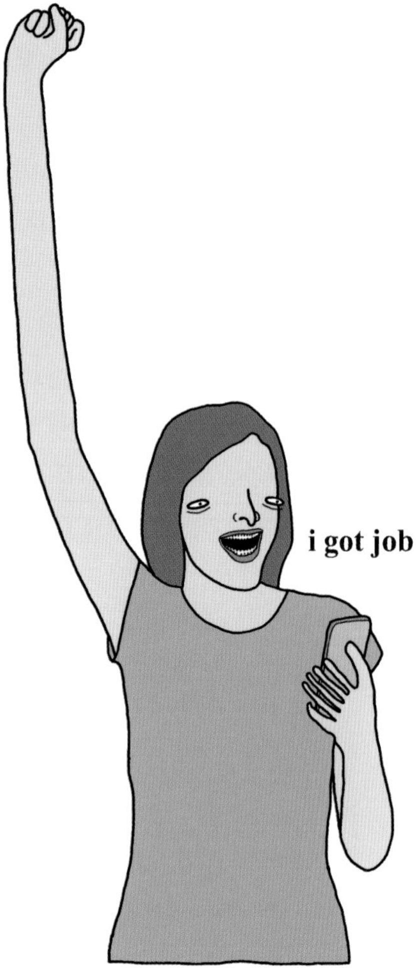
i got job

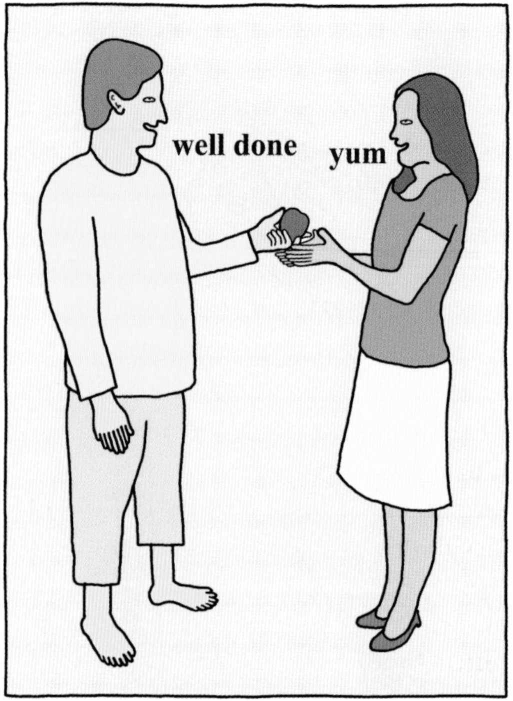
well done
yum

death

if your friend loses someone who is
close to them try and be there for them
in their time of need

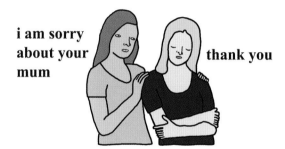

i am sorry
about your
mum

thank you

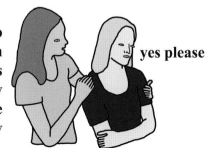

do you want me to
jump over you on
my rollerblades
like i am free willy
and you are the
little boy

yes please

free willy

losing friends

there are many ways that you can lose your friend
you can lose them in a crowd or lose them in a argument
or they can leave town or sometimes even friends will die

this is a sad part of my book but dont worry because
i think that when sadness enters your life you just have
to listen to him and ask him why he feels the way he feels
and then once you understand sadness you can be friends with
him and sometmes he will come and visit you and you will
listen to him for a while and hear what he has to say
but then he will always leave once he has told you how he feels
so be sad because there is nothing wrong with feeling that way
because sadness doesnt always stay forever
happiness will come again one day

falling out with friends

reasons that you might fall out with your friend:

• they called you a toblerone

• they said that you cant drink water out of a lake because the cup you make with your hands always has gaps in it

• they keep accusing you of stealing the pigeon eggs when you know fine well it was a eagle who took them because you saw it swoop down to get them when you was in the woods

• they keep going around telling everyone that you cant read even when you proved it to them by reading a article to them about a wolf cub in a nature magazine

• they wont text you back

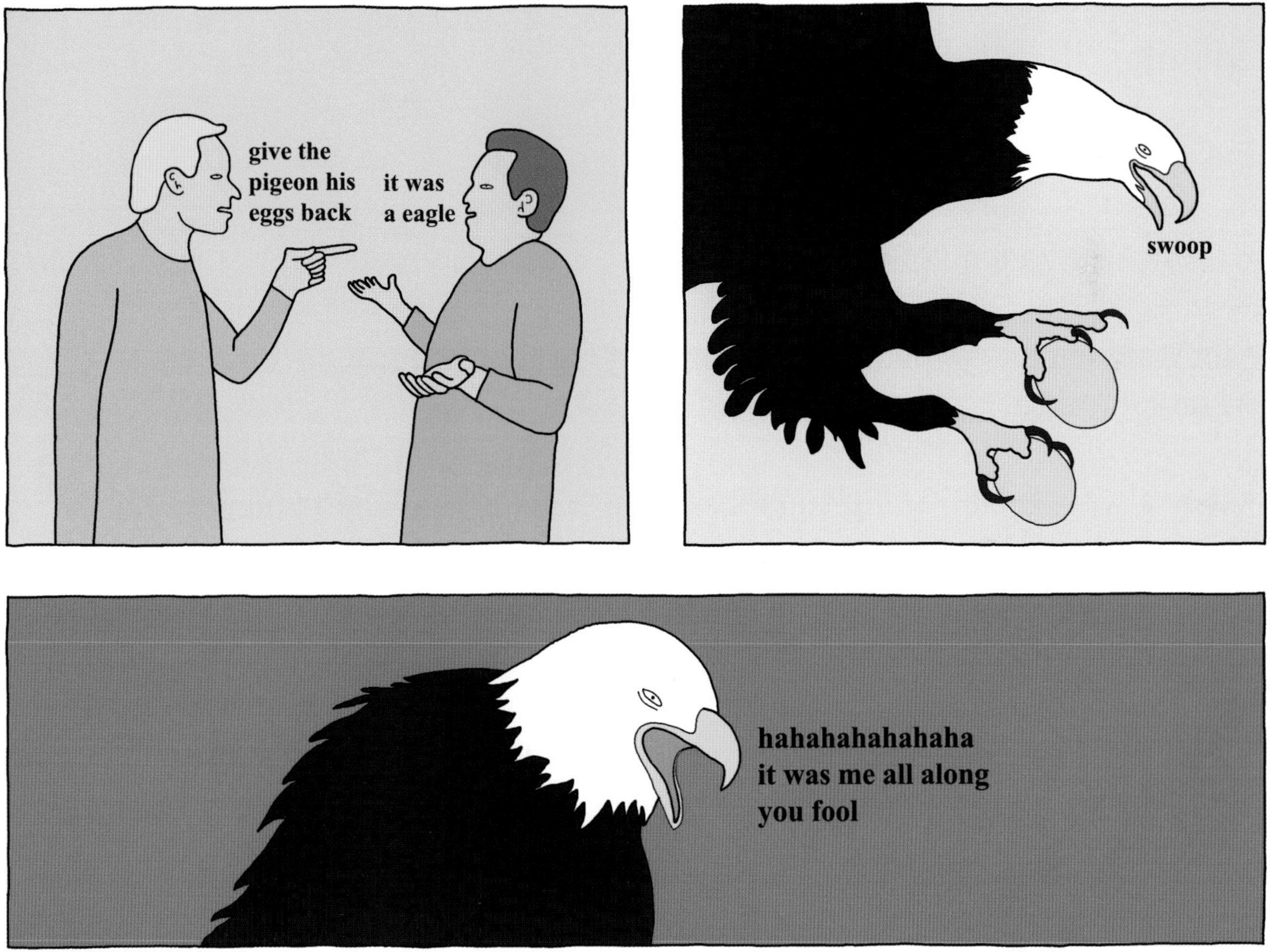
give the pigeon his eggs back
it was a eagle
swoop
hahahahahahaha it was me all along you fool

enemies

the opposite of a friend is called a enemy

reasons that you might have a enemy:

• they put a massive post on facebook saying that you say
when in rome at the wrong times

• they always post frozen soup through your letterbox when you are in bed
at night time and it stinks when it melts when you find it in the morning

• they tell everyone you are obsessed with rice

• they spread rumours about you constantly saying things like your mum
still breastfeeds you even when they know fine well i was just sleeping
on her because i fell asleep when i was having a look at her necklace

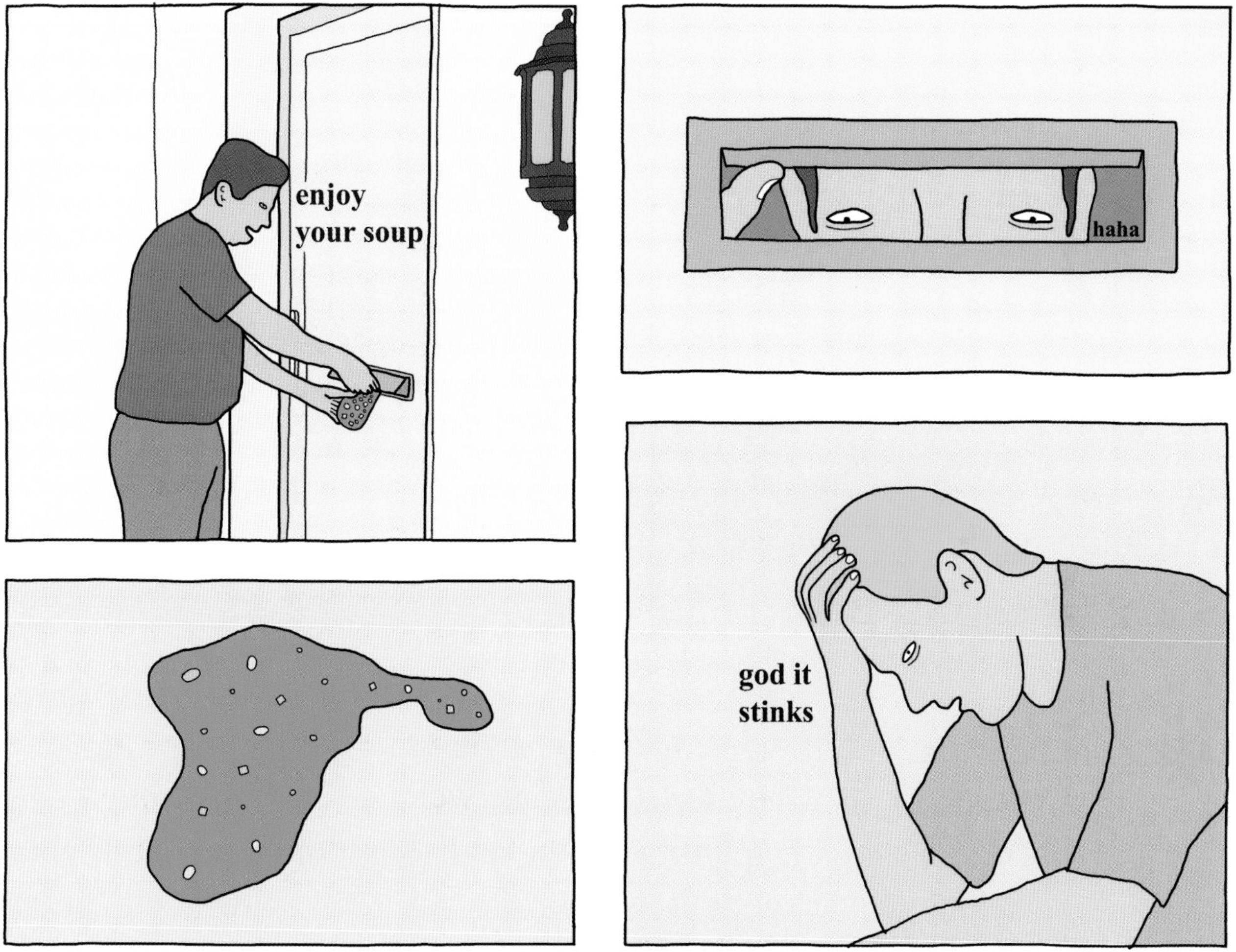
enjoy
your soup
haha
god it
stinks

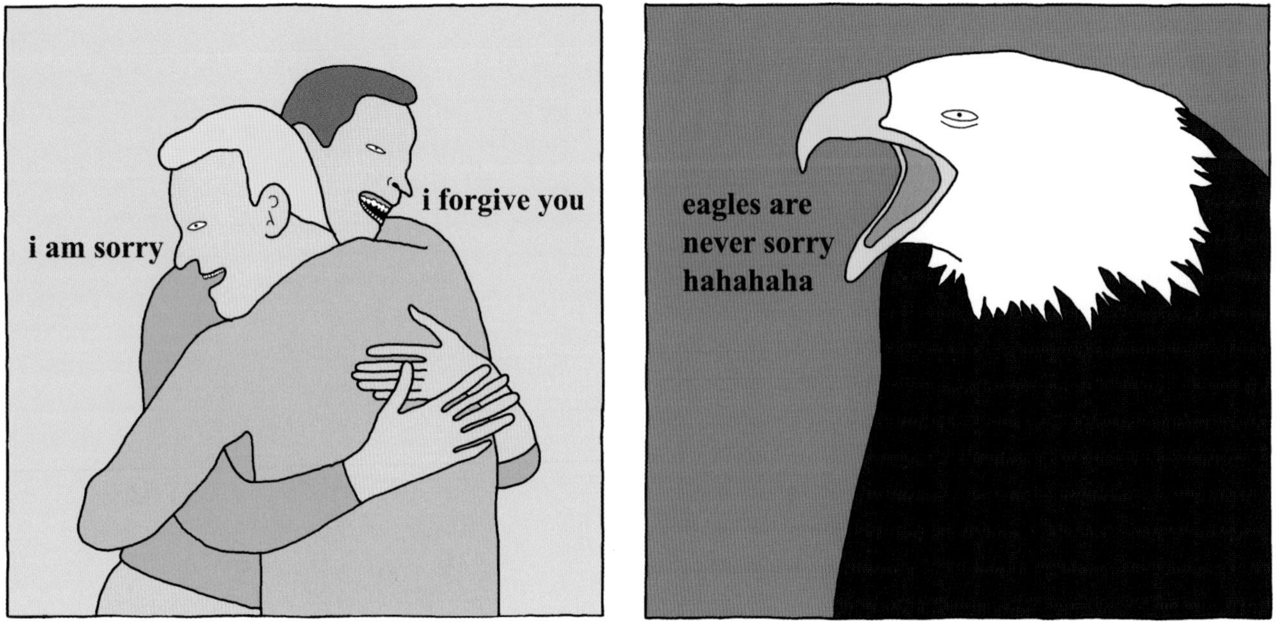
i am sorry
i forgive you
eagles are never sorry hahahaha

saying sorry

it is important to say sorry if you know that you was wrong to be mad at your friend and it is important to have a accept of your friends sorry so that you can both move on from this whole pigeon egg ordeal

moving away

sometimes a friend has to move away from where you live
this is sad because you cant be near them anymore
but the laughter you shared together will forever stay
with you inside of your heart no matter how far you are apart

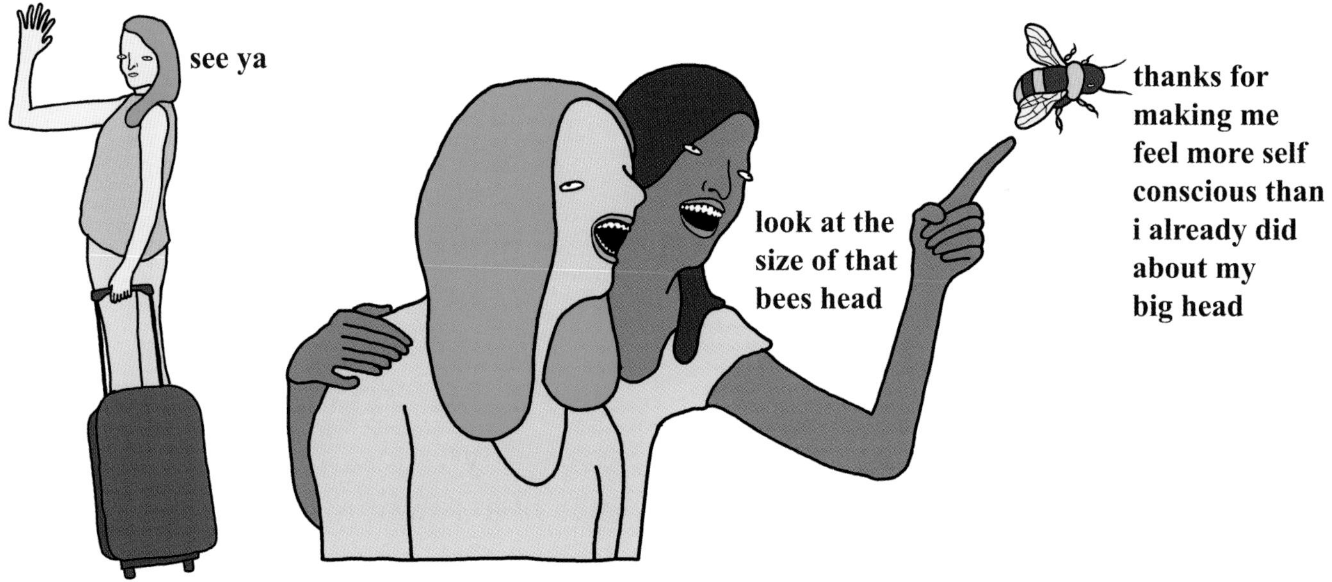
see ya
look at the size of that bees head
thanks for making me feel more self conscious than i already did about my big head

saying goodbye

one day
maybe not today or tomorrow
but one day
you will say goodbye for the last time
you might not know it in that moment
but it will be
you will remember that day
and all of the days before
but you will think about that day more
so every time you say goodbye
remember to smile
and be thankful to look into their eyes
because one day
will be your last goodbye

love from your friend
Chris (Simpsons artist) xox

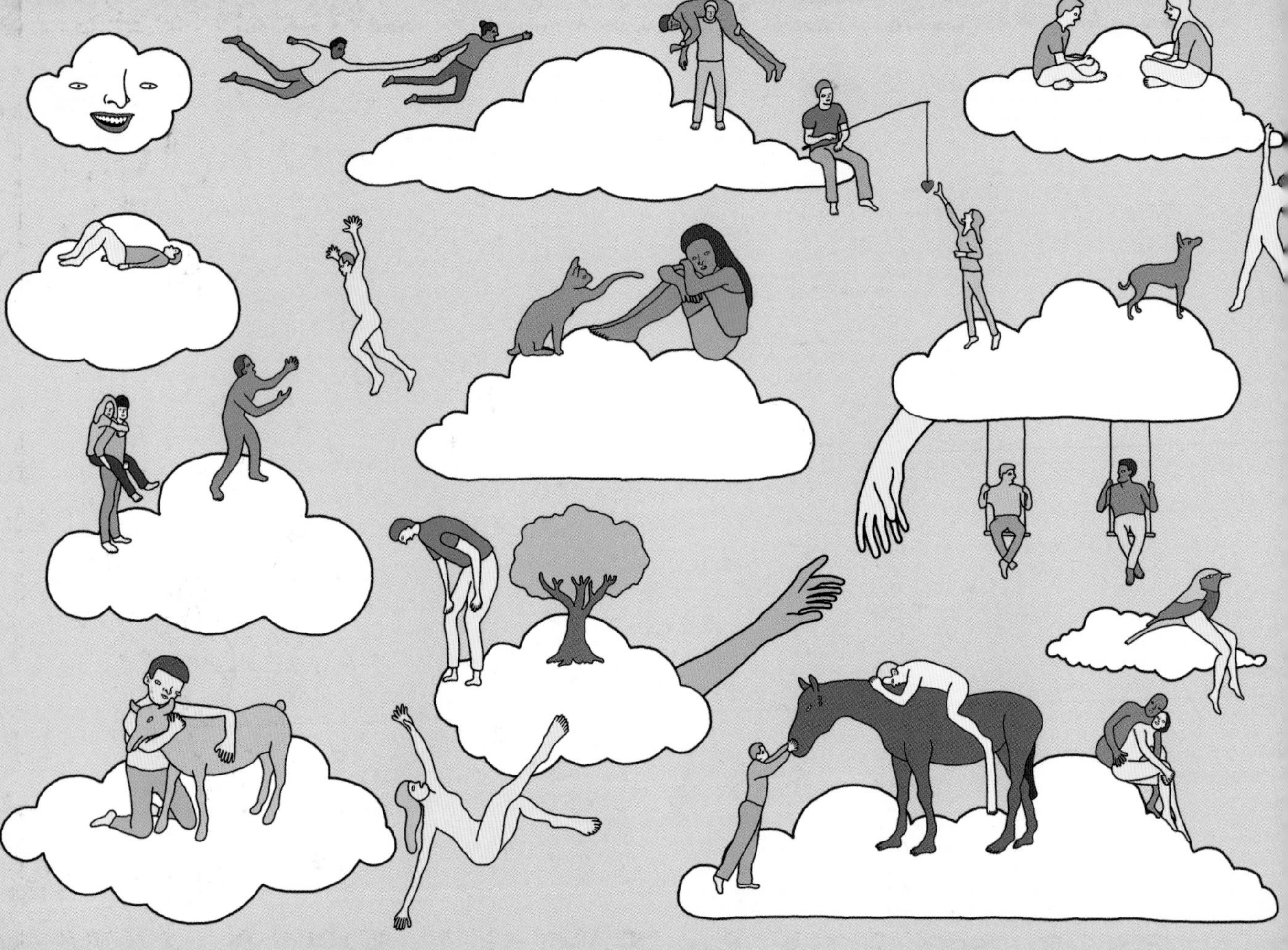